The RELICS *of* THOMAS BECKET

A True-Life Mystery

A Contribution to the 800th Anniversary of the Translation of the Relics

John Butler

The site of Thomas Becket's murder in the north-west transept of Canterbury Cathedral.

CONTENTS

PREFACE

In 1995 my book *The Quest for Becket's Bones* was published by Yale University Press. I wrote it following an intriguing story that had appeared five years earlier in the *Kentish Gazette* about two young men, Peregrine Prescott and Risto Pronk, who had been detained by security staff in the precincts of Canterbury Cathedral in the dead of night. When charged with attempted burglary, they admitted to the local magistrates that they had intended to break into the cathedral for the purpose of opening the tomb of Odet de Coligny in the Trinity Chapel. Their aim, they said, had been to prove that the relics of St Thomas Becket, which had to all intents and purposes been lost or destroyed when his shrine was dismantled on the orders of King Henry VIII in 1538, had actually been deposited in Coligny's oddly-sited tomb for safe keeping. Prescott and Pronk had planned to remove a few of the bones and subject them to an analysis that they thought would confirm their authenticity.

It quickly became apparent that the men's story had no credibility whatsoever, as they later admitted; but it served to arouse my interest in the fate of Thomas Becket's bones when they disappeared at the time of the Reformation. As I started to probe the mystery, I found myself stumbling into a chain of events which, if they had not been true, would scarcely have been credible. For almost a hundred years, from the late 1880s to the mid-1960s, a huge amount of energy was expended in high places on trying to understand what might have happened to the relics. Most of the momentum behind the quest came from successive deans and chapters of the cathedral, but other important people were also caught up in the story from time to time including an incumbent archbishop of Canterbury, a vice-chancellor of Cambridge University, an imprisoned Anglican priest, a foreign secretary, a prominent Jesuit monk from London, and a professor of anatomy at a leading London medical school.

ABOVE: St Thomas Becket, Trinity Chapel, Canterbury Cathedral, 20th century, using some medieval glass.

The appearance of *The Quest for Becket's Bones* in 1995 sparked a gratifyingly large response from many readers who offered new information or suggested further possible lines of enquiry; but once Yale University Press had decided not to publish a second edition, there was no practicable way of getting this additional material into the public domain. The 800th anniversary of the translation of St Thomas Becket's relics from his tomb in the crypt of Canterbury Cathedral to his shrine in the Trinity Chapel (in July 1220) has now given me an opportunity to update the story, and I am very grateful to Pavilion Books and the Pitkin imprint for enabling me to do so.

This book necessarily covers some of the background that first appeared in *The Quest for Becket's Bones*, for enough of the scene must be set to enable new readers who are unfamiliar with the story to

LEFT: Tomb of Odet de Coligny, Trinity Chapel, Canterbury Cathedral.

understand its context. This book does, however, include the new information that has come to light in the last twenty years, altering some of the conclusions that I had originally reached about the circumstances surrounding the destruction of Thomas Becket's shrine in 1538. It does not provide definitive answers, but I hope that it will stimulate further debate and perhaps will carry the story forwards.

I remain immensely grateful to the many people who helped me to write *The Quest for Becket's Bones* and whose names are recorded there. In addition, I would like to express my warmest thanks to Polly Powell of Pavilion Books and to Susan Swalwell and David Salmo of Pitkin Publishing for their unfailing encouragement throughout the project, and to my many friends in Canterbury who have helped me to put together the story that is told here. I am particularly grateful to Alex Palmer and Gill Butler who read and commented on the entire text in draft form; to Jim Styles who kindly allowed me to use a number of images from *The Quest for Becket's Bones*; and to Chris Needham whose encouragement over many years has always been greatly appreciated.

John Butler, Canterbury

PROLOGUE: AN ELBOW BONE

On the afternoon of 28 May 2016 a curious event occurred in the precincts of Canterbury Cathedral as a group of church and civic leaders, surrounded by interested members of the public, assembled to await the arrival of a small piece of human bone. Led by the dean and chapter (the governing body of the cathedral) in their liturgical robes, the dignitaries included the mitred Bishop of Dover with his pectoral cross and pastoral staff, the Lord Lieutenant of Kent replete with sword and tassels, and the Lord Mayor of Canterbury resplendent in the regalia of his office. The bone that they were awaiting was reputedly part of the elbow of St Thomas Becket, Canterbury's most famous archbishop who was murdered in the cathedral on 29 December 1170 by four knights from the court of King Henry II. The relic, set in a beautiful solar-shaped reliquary, was carried through the Christ Church gate and into the precincts by the Hungarian ambassador to the Court of St James accompanied by other officials from the Hungarian embassy and a small group of local pilgrims who had joined the precious object on its short journey from the nearby village of Harbledown.

ABOVE: **Basilica of the Blessed Virgin Mary, Esztergom, Hungary.**

When the two groups had met and exchanged greetings, the reliquary was carried reverently into the cathedral where it stood on the nave altar throughout a service of welcome conducted by the dean. The clergy, guests and pilgrims then processed to the crypt, passing the place in the north-west transept where Becket had been struck down in 1170, and the reliquary was placed on the altar of Our Lady Undercroft for a Roman Catholic mass. On the following day it returned to the basilica of the Blessed Virgin Mary in the Hungarian town of Esztergom, on the banks of the River Danube, where it is kept in a small backroom cupboard.

Nobody knows exactly how this piece of Thomas Becket's elbow came originally to be in Esztergom, but it is said to have been taken there by two cardinals from Hungary who were present in Canterbury Cathedral on 7 July 1220 when his tomb in the crypt was opened and the remains of his body were transferred to a newly-completed shrine in the main body of the cathedral. There is good evidence that, in the process, some small fragments of bone were kept aside and given to a few of the great churches of Europe (presumably including the basilica of Esztergom) where they were greatly revered.

The appearance of the relic in Canterbury was the culmination of an extraordinary journey it had made around London and the south-east. It arrived at Heathrow Airport on 23 May 2016 and was taken first to Westminster Cathedral where it was received at a holy mass by the President of Hungary and the Cardinal Archbishop of Westminster. On the following day the reliquary travelled

ABOVE LEFT: **Esztergom reliquary containing bone fragment of St Thomas Becket.**

ABOVE: **Limoges chasse reputed to have contained relics of St Thomas.**

to the chapel of the Mercers' Livery Company in Cheapside (the site of Becket's birthplace) for a service of celebration conducted by the Anglican Bishop of London. Over the next two days the reliquary and its bony content appeared at an evensong in Westminster Abbey, at a luncheon in the Palace of Westminster hosted by the Speaker of the House of Commons, and at St Margaret's Westminster where it was on public display. On 27 May it then journeyed to Rochester Cathedral for an overnight stop before completing the last leg of its journey to Canterbury on the following day.

This was not the first time that an important relic of St Thomas Becket had been on public display in Canterbury Cathedral. For many years a bone fragment that was described as part of the saint's finger was housed in the cathedral treasury until its removal in the early 2000s, and in 1997 a handsome 17th-century glass and silver-gilt reliquary containing a linen garment that had reputedly been worn by Becket was on display for six months, having been loaned by the Vatican. Sewn into the neckline of the garment was a 13th-century label in Latin identifying it as a 'tunicella' of Thomas Becket and sprinkled with his blood. The reliquary had been 'discovered' in 1992 in the papal Basilica of Santa Maria Maggiore in Rome where the tunicella was examined by two experts in the identification of medieval textiles, Professors Ursula Nilgen and Leonie von Wilckens of Munich University. Their report concluded that 'its authenticity can be considered a great certainty'.

Also on display in Canterbury Cathedral at the same time as the reliquary and tunicella was a 'chasse' that had reputedly once contained some bones of St Thomas. Made in the French town of Limoges in the late 12th century and loaned by the Victoria and Albert Museum (which had acquired it in 1996 from the British Rail Pension Fund), the enamelled surfaces of the chasse depicted the murder of Becket in Canterbury Cathedral on 29 December 1170 and his burial in the crypt on the following day.

Eye-catching initiatives like these by successive deans and chapters of Canterbury Cathedral have generated a great deal of public interest in the relics of St Thomas Becket, and the fate of his remains when his shrine was destroyed on the orders of King Henry VIII in September 1538 has become one of Canterbury's most enduring mysteries. 'So what happened to the bones?' is perhaps the single most frequently asked question by visitors who come to the cathedral expecting to see the archbishop's grave and are disappointed when told that nobody knows where – if anywhere – his remains are buried.

The absence of definitive evidence about the fate of Becket's bones in 1538 has not, however, prevented enquiring minds – principally those of the cathedral authorities themselves – from trying to find an answer. This book traces one strand in the endeavour that began in 1888 and continued until at least 1966. The story begins in the depths of a late 19th-century winter when Queen Victoria had just celebrated her diamond jubilee and Jack the Ripper was about to unleash his devastating assaults on the unsuspecting citizens of London's east end. In the crypt of Canterbury Cathedral two workmen were about to get a surprise.

CHAPTER 1

THE GRAVE IN THE CRYPT

On 23 January 1888, workmen who were digging in the crypt of Canterbury Cathedral uncovered a hitherto unknown grave located at the entrance to the eastern part of the crypt. According to a report that was later submitted to the dean and chapter of the cathedral, the grave contained a stone coffin, some six feet in length, that had been hewn out of a block of Portland oolite and covered with a thin slab of Merstham or Reigate firestone.[1] Although described in the report as a coffin, the vessel might more appropriately have been described as a coffer, for it was too small ever to have contained an adult body. Its width at the widest point was only fifteen inches, and a workman who tried to lie down in it was unable to do so.[2]

The coffin was buried no more than three inches beneath the level of the crypt floor, which at that time was only bare earth.[3] Its lid, which was cracked, was removed to reveal a collection of bones mixed up with earth and other debris. The arrangement of the bones in the coffin is uncertain, for modern standards of archaeological procedure were entirely absent, and several untutored hands had probably scrabbled around in the vessel before any orderly observations were made. The official report of the discovery (written by three members of the cathedral chapter who were not actually present at the time) described the bones as being gathered together 'in a heap' near the middle and one end of the coffin; but an eyewitness account by Miss Agnes Holland, the daughter of a cathedral canon who was present, told a more nuanced story.[4] She later wrote to a friend, Miss Lisa Rawlinson:

ABOVE: Mr George Austin, the Canterbury Cathedral architect who was present at the opening of the '1888 grave'.

> 'I looked down into the coffin. I perfectly remember the appearance of the skeleton. The great head lay on the slightly raised, hollowed-out, little stone pillow, and the bones were laid round the head in a sort of square. It gave a strange look. One saw the teeth.'

The bones were removed from the coffin and placed in a cardboard box that was taken to the house in the precincts of the cathedral architect, Mr George Austin. There they lay in an unused room, on deal boards covered with a grey cloth beneath a pall of white silk. Two days after the discovery the bones were shown to Dr Pugin Thornton, a member of the Royal College of Surgeons who had been called in by the dean and chapter to examine them.[5] Thornton's precise qualifications for becoming involved in the story are unclear, but his claim to be competent

LEFT: Eastern crypt of Canterbury Cathedral showing the '1888 grave' in the foreground. Becket's tomb from 1170 to 1220 was sited between the two Purbeck marble pillars.

in phrenology (a pseudo-science that purports to judge a person's character by the shape and features of the skull) may have had something to do with it. Or, as a former pupil of the King's School Canterbury, he may simply have been a local doctor who was well-known in the precincts.

Dr Thornton submitted the report of his examination of the bones to the dean and chapter in the summer of 1888.[6] He began by explaining that, by way of preparation, he had arranged the bones in their correct anatomical order (though he noted that several bones were missing), and he had mounted the several parts of the broken skull on a mound of damp modelling plaster. The resultant skeleton, Thornton concluded, was that of an adult man aged between about 45 and 55. The long bones suggested that he had been of considerable height – 'probably six feet two inches'. The reconstructed skull was large, some 22.75 inches in circumference, and the right side had been fractured by a blow that, in Thornton's opinion, might have been caused by a mace or a pickaxe. The left side had sustained a much greater injury. The report noted a gaping wound of five to six inches in length extending from a line drawn upwards from behind the ear to the centre of the forehead. Since the upper edge of the wound was an almost perfect straight line, Thornton concluded that it might have been caused by a blow from a heavy cutting instrument such as a two-handed sword. The blow could not have been inflicted after death, for otherwise the dried-out plates of the skull would simply have shattered.

The bones were kept in Mr Austin's house for sixteen days, during which time they were seen by a number of people, among them Father John Morris, a prominent Jesuit monk from the Farm Street community in London who twice made the journey to Canterbury and who became a vigorous contributor to the heated debate that soon erupted about the identification of the bones.[7] Rumours that they might be the long-lost bones of St Thomas Becket must have arisen and spread almost immediately, for a man from Margate came with his blind son who was allowed to place his eyes close to the orbital sockets of the skull and was told by his father: 'Now, no doctors can heal you; you must pray for yourself.'[8] The outcome is unrecorded.

BECKET'S BONES.

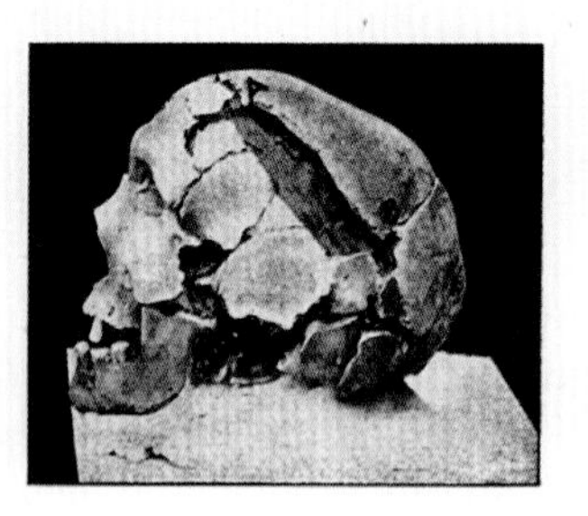

BY

W. PUGIN THORNTON,

AUTHOR OF

"*Phrenology; or, Heads and what they tell us.*"

Price—ONE SHILLING.

ABOVE: Title page of Dr Pugin Thornton's pamphlet *Becket's Bones*, published in 1901.

The bones were reinterred in the grave in the eastern crypt at 3.30 in the afternoon of 10 February 1888.[9] Once again the little ceremony was witnessed and reported upon by the vigilant Agnes Holland. An oak container had been fashioned to sit inside the stone vessel, and the bones were returned to it. The skull, still affixed around Dr Thornton's clay mould, was replaced on the stone cushion on which it had been found and the long bones were arranged around it. A glass bottle containing a photograph of the skull and an account of Thornton's findings were placed next to it, and when everything had been returned the coffin was sealed with a new stone slab weighing 15 hundredweight. Miss Holland observed:

> 'I murmured softly in the Dean's ear, "Mr Dean, wouldn't it be very nice if something was made to mark out the place? Some pavement round you know, tiles or something?" "Oh yes. Something we will have."'[10]

But nothing was done.

---

[1] C.F. Routledge, J.B. Sheppard and W.A. Scott Robertson, 'The Crypt of Canterbury Cathedral', *Archaeologia Cantiana*, XVIII, 1889, pp. 253–256.

[2] A.J. Mason, *What Became of the Bones of St Thomas?*, Cambridge, 1920, p. 181.

[3] Routledge et al, *op cit*, p. 253.

[4] Miss Holland's correspondence with Miss Rawlinson is reproduced in Mason, *op cit*, pp. 175–182.

[5] W.P. Thornton, letter to *The Times*, 16 February 1888. Thornton was a nephew of the celebrated gothic architect Augustus Welby Pugin.

[6] W.P. Thornton, 'Surgical Report on a Skeleton Found in the Crypt of Canterbury Cathedral', *Archaeologia Cantiana*, XVIII, 1889, pp. 257–260.

[7] Fr J. Morris, letters to *The Times*, 10 February, 20 February, 28 February and 16 March 1888.

[8] Mason, *op cit*, p. 179; W.P. Thornton, *Becket's Bones*, Canterbury, 1901, p. 6.

[9] H.G. Austin, letter to *The Times*, 15 February 1888.

[10] A. Holland, quoted in Mason, *op cit*, p. 180. The dean at the time was Dr Robert Payne-Smith.

CHAPTER 2

THOMAS BECKET: IN LIFE AND IN DEATH

ABOVE: Late 12th-century fresco of the murder of Thomas Becket, Church of SS Giovanni e Paolo, Spoleto, Italy.

As the visit of the Margate man and his blind son attests, the possibility was present from the moment the bones were found in 1888 that they might be those of Canterbury's martyred archbishop, St Thomas Becket. News of the curious goings-on in the cathedral crypt was reported in both local and national newspapers, and the question buzzing busily around the cathedral precincts in the aftermath of the find was not 'whose bones are they?' but 'are they the bones of Thomas Becket?' The circumstances of the find, together with Dr Pugin Thornton's report of his examination of the skeleton, provided a good deal of seemingly convincing evidence in support of a positive answer to the question; but to understand why this was so it is necessary to turn the clock back from 1888; first to 1170, then to 1220, and then to 1538.

Thomas Becket, the thirty-ninth archbishop of Canterbury, was born in Cheapside in about 1120, the son of a wealthy London merchant.[1] He was able, ambitious and well-educated, and in his twenties he began to work in the household of the then archbishop of Canterbury, Theobald. Impressed with Becket's sharp mind and engaging personality, Theobald sent him to study canon law in Europe, and in 1154 he became archdeacon of Canterbury. Becket's swift rise continued in the following year when, having been commended by Theobald to King Henry II, he joined the king's household as chancellor of England.

Though separated by a vast social chasm the two men forged a strong personal as well as political relationship. Indeed, Henry came to rely so much upon his chancellor's administrative and diplomatic skills that when Theobald died in 1161 the king chose Becket to succeed him. Henry's motives were largely self-interested. He had come to see the English church as a threat to his customary rights as king, and in Becket he believed he had a trusted ally with whom he could do business. He could not have been more wrong, for as soon as Becket became God's man, his loyalty lay with the church. From the day of his enthronement in 1162 Becket made plain his determination to protect the privileges of the English church from Henry's attempts to annexe its wealth and limit its jurisdictional powers, and the two men who had once been almost as close as brothers quickly became bitter adversaries.

Thomas Becket's eight years as archbishop of Canterbury, most of which were spent in exile in France, were marked by increasingly angry confrontations with the king. Matters came to a head in December 1170 when Henry, celebrating Christmas with his court at Bur-le-Roi in Normandy, finally snapped. Furious at the continuation of Becket's defiance of his royal authority,

ABOVE: St Thomas Becket in conversation with King Henry II, manuscript by Peter Langtoft, 1300.

LEFT: Trinity Chapel, Canterbury Cathedral, showing the candle that marks the site of Becket's shrine from 1220 to 1538.

he cursed the knights of his court as 'a nest of cowards and traitors who had allowed their lord to be treated with contempt by a low-born priest'. Hearing these words, four knights of the court slipped out, determined to please the king by silencing Becket. They rode to Canterbury, and in the late afternoon of 29 December they confronted the archbishop inside the cathedral. After a brief and furious exchange of words, the knights drew their swords and struck Becket violently about his head and shoulders, killing him instantly and opening up a large wound in his head through which blood and brains oozed out onto the floor. Satisfied that he would not rise again, they made their escape through the door into the cloisters by which they had entered.

News of Thomas Becket's murder in Canterbury Cathedral in 1170 spread rapidly throughout Europe, reaching as far afield as Iceland and Sicily (where a very early mosaic depiction of the saint is still to be seen beside the high altar in the cathedral of Monreale in Palermo). Consequences soon followed. Becket was declared a martyr for the Catholic church, and in 1173 he was canonised by Pope Callixtus III as St Thomas of Canterbury. There is evidence that the four knights may have been banished to the crusader kingdom of Jerusalem where they probably died within a few years.[2] As for King Henry II, he made a spectacular pilgrimage of contrition to Canterbury in 1174, walking barefoot through the city to the cathedral where he was scourged by the monks before fasting in prayer for twenty-four hours at Becket's tomb.

For the first fifty years following his death, Becket's body lay in a simple tomb at the eastern end of the crypt; but on 7 July 1220, in one of the great religious gatherings of medieval Catholic Europe, presided over by Archbishop Stephen Langton and attended by the young King Henry III, his holy relics were taken from the tomb in the crypt and placed inside a magnificent gilded and bejewelled shrine that had been constructed in the newly completed Trinity Chapel at the eastern extremity of the cathedral. It became known as the festival of the 'translation of the relics',[3] and for the next three hundred or so years Canterbury was among the most important pilgrimage centres in Europe as noblemen and peasants alike flocked to Becket's shrine in search of salvation and healing. Aided by Geoffrey Chaucer's iconic *Canterbury Tales* in the late 14th century, the city became both famous and rich on account of the terrible event that had occurred there in December 1170.

The pilgrimages to Becket's shrine finally ended in 1538 as the particular effects of the European Reformation, begun in Germany by Martin Luther in 1517, started to be felt in England. In 1534, under the Act of Supremacy, King Henry VIII took the English church away from the authority of the pope in Rome and declared himself to be its supreme governor. The reasons were various, but prominent among them was the refusal of Pope Clement VII to allow him to divorce his first wife, Catherine of Aragon. As if to underscore his break from Rome, Henry hit out at two of the bastions of Roman Catholic piety: the monasteries and the cult of the saints. In the space of little more than a decade between 1530 and 1540 all the English monasteries were closed and the shrines of all but one of the English saints were destroyed (the

Prima. pars
Here begynneth the Segge of Thebes ful
lamentably tolde by Iohn lidgate Monke of
Bury annexynge it to ye talys of Cauntbury
Sirs quod I. sith of youre Curtesye
I entrede am · in to youre Companye
And admytted · a tale for to telle
By hym that hath power to compelle
I mene oure hoste governere and gyde
Of yow echeone · rydinge here by syde
Though my wit. bareyne be and dulle
I wolle reherce · a storry wonderfulle
Touchinge the segge · and destruccyoun
Of worthy Thebes · the myghty royalle Toun
Bilt and bygonne · of olde antiquite
Upon the tyme · of worthy Iosue
By diligence · of kynge Amphioun
Cheeff cause first · of this foundacioun

exception being that of King Edward the Confessor at Westminster). The impact of these two actions on the social, economic and religious fabric of the country was immense.

Canterbury's turn came late in the day, but in September 1538 the shrines of the six saints that had stood in the cathedral for centuries (Wilfrid, Oda, Dunstan, Alphege, Anselm and Becket) were dismantled and their jewels and precious metals were taken to the royal treasury in the Tower of London. That much is certain; but exactly what happened to the relics is far less clear. No general instructions had been issued about the way in which the bones of the unshrined saints should be treated,[4] and no specific mandate appears to have been given for the disposal of the relics at Canterbury.[5] In most places where the outcome is known, the bones of the saints were buried discreetly but reverently in places where they could no longer act as foci of Catholic piety. The same might have happened to the bones of St Thomas when they were removed from the shrine; but in his case stories quickly arose that something different had been done to them: they had been burnt. The details of the story varied from one telling to another. In some versions the bones had been incinerated inside the cathedral, in others they had been cast

ABOVE LEFT: Artist's impression of Becket's shrine in the Trinity Chapel, Canterbury Cathedral.

ABOVE: Pilgrims on the road, from *The Canterbury Tales* by Geoffrey Chaucer.

into a fire in the streets of Canterbury. In some versions the ashes from the blaze had been thrown to the winds, in others they had been scattered on the waters of the nearby River Stour, and in yet others they had been fired through the barrel of a cannon.

Self-evidently, these stories could not all have been true, and it was precisely because no one knew exactly what had happened to the relics of Thomas Becket that, as soon as the 1888 bones had been reinterred in their grave in the eastern crypt, a fierce debate erupted about their provenance. Were they the long-lost relics of St Thomas or weren't they? It quickly became apparent that this was more than a question of passing antiquarian interest.

RIGHT: **King Henry VIII, who ordered the destruction of Becket's shrine in 1538.**

---

[1] There are many biographies of Thomas Becket. The material in this chapter is based largely on F. Barlow, *Thomas Becket*, London, 1986.

[2] N. Vincent, *Becket's Murderers*, Canterbury, 2004, p. 25.

[3] There are several accounts of the translation of the relics in July 1220. The *Polistorie*, a Canterbury chronicle in French, is generally regarded as bearing the stamp of accuracy. It is summarised in A.J. Mason, *What Became of the Bones of St Thomas?*, Cambridge, 1920. The *Quadrilogus*, a 13th-century conflation of five separate biographies of Becket, is summarised in Barlow, *op cit.*

[4] Mason, *op cit*, p. 123.

[5] H.S. Milman, 'The Vanished Memorials of St Thomas of Canterbury', *Archaeologia*, 53, part 1, 1892, p. 219.

CHAPTER 3

ARE THEY BECKET'S BONES?

Given what was – and was not – known in 1888 about the fate of Thomas Becket's relics when his shrine was dismantled at the time of the Reformation, there were a number of striking features about the bones discovered in the crypt of Canterbury Cathedral that led many people instantly to conclude that they could indeed be those of the saint. To the question 'Are they Becket's bones?' some were all too keen to answer 'Yes'; and there seemed to be good reasons for doing so.[1]

First, there was the location of the grave: immediately in line with, and only a few steps away from, the site of Becket's original tomb in the eastern crypt where his body had lain for fifty years between his death in December 1170 and the translation of his relics to the shrine in the Trinity Chapel in July 1220. The grave was therefore in a special place, intimately associated with the saint and – assuming it had been created later than 1170 – unlikely to have been chosen as the burial site of any lesser mortal.

Second, the coffin had been buried only a few inches beneath the surface of the crypt floor. Even allowing for the fact that the water table beneath the crypt is quite high, it still seemed a very odd finding. Of course, the point did not go unremarked that if the monks had had word of the imminent arrival of King Henry's commissioners in September 1538 and had removed the relics from the shrine before they turned up at the cathedral, a secret burial might well have had to be arranged, with very little time to excavate a grave to the normal depth. A hasty burial only a few inches beneath the surface would have had to suffice for the purpose.

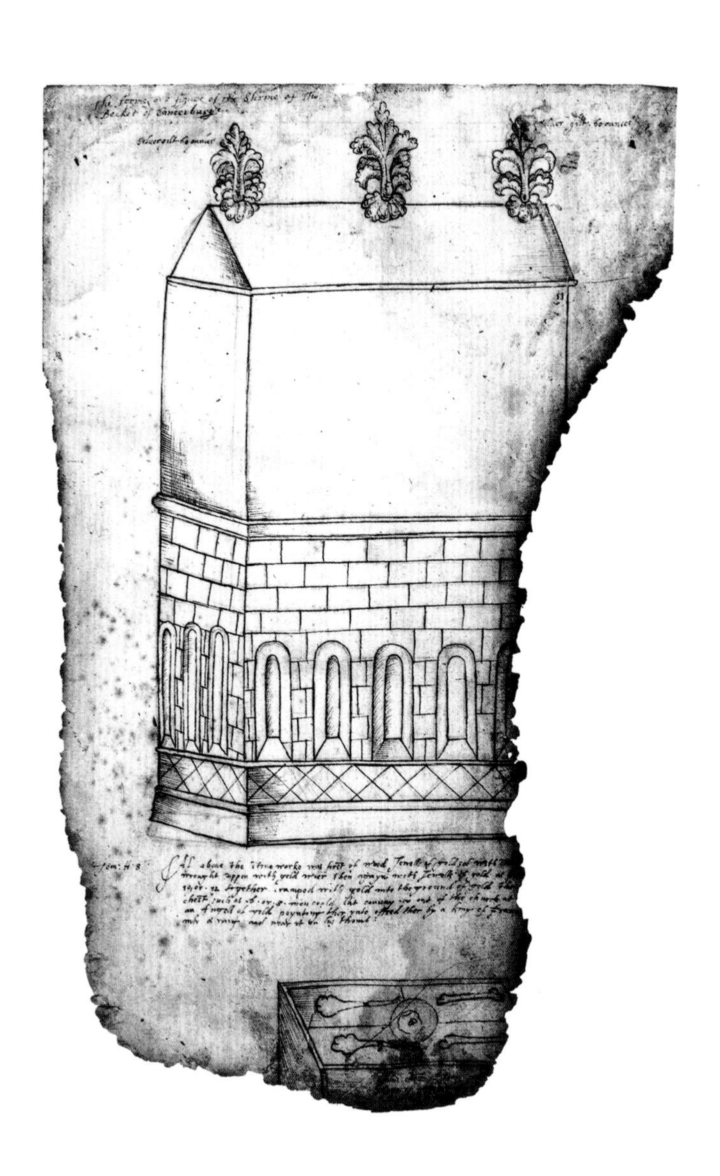

ABOVE: Partially destroyed 16th-century drawing of Becket's shrine in the Cotton Manuscripts.

Third, there was no doubt that the coffin had never contained a body. Not only was it too narrow to accommodate the workman who tried to lie down in it, there was no suggestion by those who were present that the bones it contained were arranged in the form of a human skeleton. They had clearly been placed there as bones taken from somewhere else, not as a human body from which the flesh had subsequently rotted away. This, too, struck many people as highly significant, for what would have been removed from Becket's shrine at, or just before, its destruction in 1538 would have been loose bones, not an intact body.

Fourth, the observation of Miss Agnes Holland about the arrangement of the bones in the coffin was also extremely suggestive.[2] What she said she saw was almost ritualistic in nature, with the skull lying on a stone cushion and other bones arranged around it 'in a sort of square'. Although there is no definitive account of the way that Becket's bones were laid out inside his shrine, there is a 16th-century illustration among the Cotton Manuscripts in the British Library that purports to show just that.[3] In the drawing, the skull sits centrally on a sort of platform, with the long bones arranged around it.[4] The inscription accompanying the drawing was partially destroyed by fire in 1731, but it had earlier been recorded by the Tudor chronicler John Stow, who had presumably seen the manuscripts in their undamaged form.[5]

> 'This chest of iron contained the bones of Thomas Becket, skull and all, with the wounde of his death and the pece cut out of his skull laid in the same wounde.'

The Cotton Manuscripts were well known in the late 19th century, and the similarities between the drawing and Miss Holland's observation of the way the bones were arranged in the coffin in the crypt, particularly the treatment of the skull, struck many people as beyond the

BELOW: Two photographs of Thornton's reconstruction of the '1888 skull' that were taken before its reinterment.

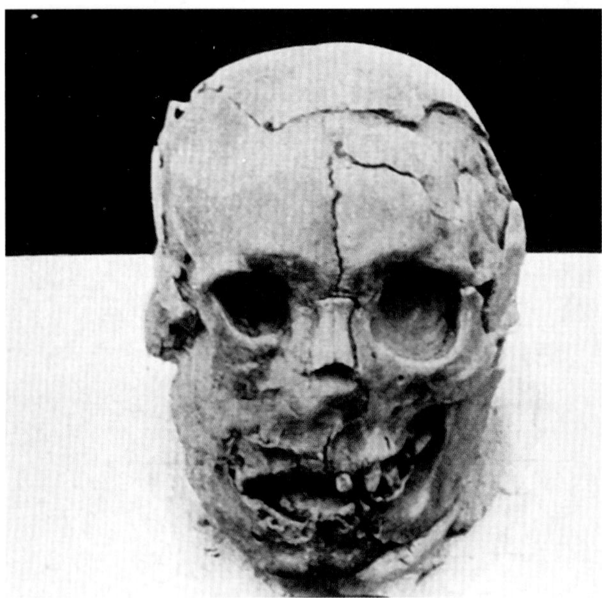

possibility of coincidence. Whoever had placed the bones in the coffin *must* have known how Becket's relics had been laid out in the shrine and had deliberately tried to replicate it. There could surely be no other explanation for what would otherwise have been a bizarre arrangement.

Fifth, Dr Pugin Thornton's examination of the bones during the short time they were on the surface concluded that they had belonged to a large man aged between about 45 and 55. These characteristics fitted Thomas Becket very well: he was about fifty at the time of his death, and the contemporary chronicles concur that he was of unusually large height. He may even have been taller than the six feet and two inches that Thornton attributed to the skeleton; but at least his observation was pointing in the right direction.

Finally, Dr Thornton's reconstruction of the pieces of the skull, modelled on the clay mould, revealed a gaping wound that was dramatically consistent with the contemporary accounts of Becket's murder at the hands of his assailants in December 1170. One of the several sword-blows that rained down upon him landed on his head, opening up a large wound in the skull through which tissue and blood from his brain oozed out onto the floor. Thornton's discovery of a clean-edged fracture, at precisely the point where the strike from a right-handed assailant would probably have landed if aimed at Becket's head, seemed to be more than mere coincidence. Thornton had, admittedly, exceeded his brief in suggesting that the fracture could have been caused by a heavy two-handed sword, but the photographic evidence was clearly there for others to draw their own conclusions.[6]

In view of all of this, it is hardly surprising that once Dr Thornton's report had come into the public domain in 1889, many felt the case to be cut and dried that the long-lost relics of St Thomas of Canterbury had finally been unearthed. Not everyone agreed, however, and from the moment the bones were reinterred in the grave in the eastern crypt in February 1888 a fierce national debate broke out between those who *were* sure that they were the bones of the saint – the 'believers' – and those who were equally sure that they *weren't* – the 'sceptics'. The course of the debate over the next sixty years was dramatically to demonstrate both the hope and the fear that Thomas Becket could still inspire in the hearts and minds of many in the Church of England centuries after his brutal death.

---

[1] The information in this Chapter is drawn from the two official reports submitted to the dean and chapter in 1888. They were published as: C.F. Routledge, J.B. Sheppard and W.A. Scott Robertson, 'The Crypt of Canterbury Cathedral', *Archaeologia Cantiana*, XVIII, 1889, pp. 253–256 and W.P. Thornton, 'Surgical Report on a Skeleton Found in the Crypt of Canterbury Cathedral', *Archaeologia Cantiana*, XVIII, 1889, pp. 257-260.

[2] Miss Holland's correspondence with Miss Lisa Rawlinson is reproduced in A.J. Mason, *What Became of the Bones of St Thomas?*, Cambridge, 1920, pp. 175–182.

[3] British Library, Cotton MS, Tib. E, VIII, fol. 269.

[4] The drawing is reproduced in A.P. Stanley, *Historical Memorials of Canterbury*, London, 1912 (11th edition), facing p. 291 and R. Strong, *Lost Treasures of Britain*, London, 1990, p. 28.

[5] For a fuller account of the illustration of the Cotton Manuscript and the deciphering of the inscription, see Stanley, *op cit*, p. 291.

[6] Three photographs of the skull were reproduced in W.P. Thornton, *Becket's Bones*, Canterbury, 1901.

CHAPTER 4

BELIEVERS AND SCEPTICS

ABOVE: Bishop Edward King of Lincoln.

On 25 January 1888, just two days after the discovery of the bones in the eastern crypt of Canterbury Cathedral, a new reredos was unveiled in St Paul's Cathedral in London.[1] Made of marble and topped by a statue of the Virgin Mary, it enclosed the largest crucifix to appear in an Anglican church since the Reformation. It was designed by G. F. Bodley, the renowned Gothic revivalist architect, and its appearance sent shock waves through many middle-of-the-road Anglicans who saw in its dominance and emotional intensity yet further evidence of a gradual shift within the Church of England towards Roman Catholicism. By now the Anglo-Catholic Oxford movement had reached the summit of its influence in the church, and many of its leaders were busily transforming its culture and rituals. Among them were Richard Church and Henry Liddon, friends and associates of John Henry Newman and Edward Pusey, whose appointments to the chapter of St Paul's Cathedral in the early 1870s had caused alarm bells to sound in low-church quarters. Even Queen Victoria seemed well-disposed towards Rome, willingly acceding to a Vatican request for a papal envoy to be formally admitted to her jubilee celebrations in 1887.

A symbolically important event occurred three years later, in 1890, when the bishop of Lincoln, Edward King, was charged with ritual offences under the Public Worship Regulation Act of 1874.[2] The bishop had allegedly allowed Anglo-Catholic rituals to be enacted in his diocese, among them the mixing of communion wine and water and the signing of the cross at the absolution. The case was heard in an ecclesiastical court by the Archbishop of Canterbury, Edward White Benson, who found King guilty on two counts of ritualism but allowed the continuation of other practices including the use of altar candles and the mixing of wine and water. Edward King was by no means a militant Anglo-Catholic, but in an age when the cry of 'no popery here' could still arouse strong passions, deep concern was felt among many Protestants that a high-level conspiracy might be afoot to move the English church closer to Rome.

It is in this ecclesiastical context that the significance of the bones found in the bowels of the mother church of Anglicanism and believed by many to be the relics of the greatest of the English Catholic saints should be understood. These were not just any ancient bones: they were little short of political dynamite. If they really were the long-lost relics of St Thomas, then who could tell what the outcome might be for future relations between Canterbury and Rome? Would Rome ask for its relics back? Would there be a demand for the Catholic mass to be celebrated in the cathedral on Becket's festival days in July and December? Would there be a revival of the

LEFT: The 19th-century Bodley reredos in St Paul's Cathedral.

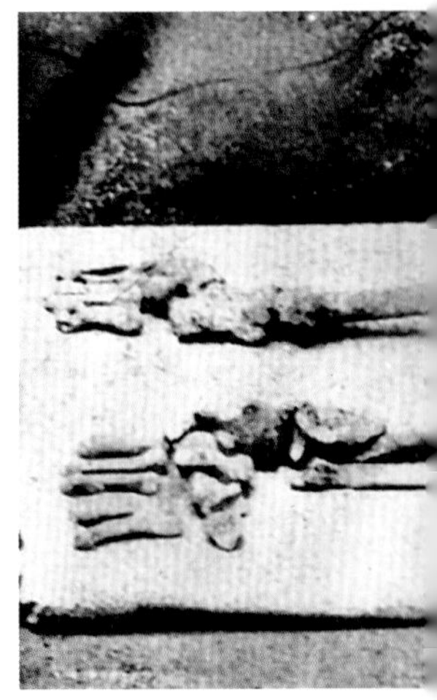

medieval pilgrimages? Would the blind and the lame flock to Canterbury once again in search of miracles? Might Canterbury even become the Lourdes of England? The stakes were perilously high, and many of those on both sides of the debate about the 1888 grave saw in the bones only what they wanted to see. A balanced view was very hard to come by.

The debate between the 'believers' and the 'sceptics' was conducted on a broad canvas and lasted for several decades.[3] It was confined mainly to churchmen, politicians, antiquarians and historians, but ordinary members of the public also weighed in from time to time. The channels through which the debate was conducted were also varied, including letters to national newspapers, journal articles, talks to learned societies and even, in at least one case, a pulpit sermon. Many different positions emerged as claim and counter-claim reverberated among the participants; but by about 1920 the salient points on both sides of the argument had been rehearsed *ad nauseam* and there was little to be said that was genuinely new. It didn't help, of course, that nobody could actually go back and re-examine the bones: they had been reinterred in February 1888 after only sixteen days on the surface, and everything that was known about them was contained in Dr Pugin Thornton's report to the dean and chapter and the handful of photographs that had been taken at the time. Inevitably in such circumstances, faith and hope mingled with objectivity and evidence to produce a multi-hued tapestry of public and specialist opinion in which fact could rarely be separated from supposition and nobody could be certain they were right.

The 'believers' in the debate relied heavily on Dr Thornton's findings to support their case. His conclusion that the bones had been those of a tall man of late middle age whose skull had been cloven with what could have been a heavy blow from a double-handed sword seemed very persuasive. When to this was added the highly significant location of the grave, the shallow depth of the burial, and the likelihood that the bones had been arranged in the coffin in the same way that Becket's relics had been laid out in his shrine, the case seemed overwhelming. Taken together, these things could surely not have been coincidental.

To press their case, however, the 'believers' also had to explain how the relics could have survived the despoliation of the shrine at the hands of Henry VIII's commissioners in 1538. That there was no authentic record of what had happened to the saint's bones was actually an advantage to them, for explanations could be concocted that the 'sceptics' were unable to refute with solid evidence. Much was made by the 'believers' of documented events elsewhere, particularly in monastic settings where the shrines of prominent local saints had been dismantled on the orders of the king. It was not unusual in these places for relics to be moved around for their safe-keeping,[4] and in some churches the monks were even said to have hidden them and replaced them with substitute bones for the king's commissioners to find and deal with in the approved manner.[5]

BELOW: **A photograph of the '1888 skeleton' that was taken before its reinterment.**

Some such trickery *could* have happened at Canterbury where the relics of St Thomas were of such overwhelming spiritual significance for the monks of the cathedral that it was all but impossible to imagine them waiting passively for their destruction at the hands of a tyrant king – a king, moreover, who might not have much longer to live and who might then be succeeded by his Catholic daughter, Mary Tudor. All that was needed was for tonsures to remain below the parapet and await the Catholic restoration that would surely come, for there was no reason to suppose that the reforms initiated by a physically ailing king would hold any sway in the long term.

The 'sceptics' were unimpressed by all of this. They pointed out – correctly – that no proper observations had been made or records kept when the coffin had first been opened in 1888, and nobody could be sure of the exact arrangement of its contents. Moreover, Dr Thornton's report to the dean and chapter was riddled with guesses, estimates and suppositions. He was an unreliable witness who had exceeded his brief. On the question of whether the relics of Thomas Becket could have survived the destruction of his shrine in 1538, the 'sceptics' were brutal in their dismissal of any arguments in its favour. Becket, they pointed out, was not like any of the other English saints: in the eyes of King Henry VIII he was a traitor who had defied the royal prerogative of another king of England, and all references to him in the church's calendars and liturgies were soon to be violently obliterated. To suppose that the monks of Christ Church would have dared to risk life and limb in the face of such implacable hostility was simply ridiculous. It couldn't have happened.

In support of their claims, the 'sceptics' pointed to a number of more-or-less contemporary documents that seemed, at face value, to prove that Becket's bones had been burnt on the spot and the ashes scattered to the winds or strewn across the waters of a local river.[6] Some of these documents, especially those that had originated with Pope Paul III in Rome, appeared to have come with impeccable credentials and had to be taken seriously; but they all contained an impediment that could not be wished away, for even if bones *had* been burnt at the time the shrine was destroyed, they could not conclusively be shown to have been those of Becket. The evidence was simply not there. Indeed, as the 'believers' were all too ready to point out, they could just as well have been substitute bones that had been placed in the shrine for the king's commissioners to find and destroy.

By the end of the Great War in 1918 the debate about the identity of the bones that had been discovered thirty years earlier had reached a stalemate. Amidst claim and counter-claim, very little could be pinned down and positions were becoming ever more entrenched. Yet the questions would not go away, and as the Church of England embarked upon what turned out to be a long and tortuous attempt to revise the Book of Common Prayer (another cause of friction between high-church and low-church factions), a goodly number of people in Anglicanism were still obsessed with the bones in the crypt of Canterbury cathedral and the potential that they held for their politico-ecclesiastical ambitions. Something had to be done – and it took the Archbishop of Canterbury to do it.

---

[1] O. Chadwick, *The Victorian Church*, Part II, London, 1972, p. 352. The reredos, which was consecrated on 29 June 1888, was largely destroyed in the Second World War, though the figure of the crucified Christ still remains in the possession of the cathedral.

[2] *Oxford Dictionary of National Biography*, 2004, article on Bishop Edward King.

[3] For a full account of the course of the debate see J. R. Butler, *The Quest for Becket's Bones*, Yale, 1995, Chapters 3 and 4.

[4] J. Bentley, *Restless Bones*, London, 1985.

[5] D. Willem, *St Cuthbert's Corpse: A Life After Death*, Durham, 2013.

[6] The evidence for the burning of Becket's bones is considered in greater detail in Chapter 9.

CHAPTER 5

ARCHIEPISCOPAL INTERVENTION

It is not clear why the archbishop of Canterbury, Randall Thomas Davidson, should have intervened at this stage in the debate about the bones in the crypt, but he did. It was a controversial step to take, for it drew the nation's attention to something that many in the Church of England would have preferred to remain hidden. Davidson was arguably the most politically astute of all the 20th-century archbishops of Canterbury,[1] and he would not have intervened without good reason; but whether he was acting entirely of his own volition or was responding to representations that had been made to him has never been clarified.

At some time before 1920 Davidson commissioned Canon Arthur James Mason to 'bring together all the relevant documents bearing upon the question of whether the bones discovered in the crypt of Canterbury Cathedral in 1888 could be those of St Thomas Becket'. The archbishop's choice of Mason was a clear indication of the seriousness with which he took the matter, for Mason came with impeccable credentials.[2] A Cambridge graduate in his late sixties, he had earlier been diocesan missioner at Truro Cathedral, Lady Margaret professor of divinity at Cambridge, and Master of Pembroke College. Towards the end of his career in 1908 he was appointed Vice-Chancellor of Cambridge University, a post that he held for three years before retiring to Canterbury where he was made an honorary canon and where he died in 1928. A traditionalist by instinct, Arthur Mason was a welcome and trusted figure in the corridors of Anglican power without ever being the archbishop's poodle – an ideal position from which to investigate the bones in the crypt.

ABOVE: Archbishop Randall Thomas Davidson, by Leslie Ward.

Mason gave every impression of coming to his task with an open mind. He inclined towards the higher end of the spectrum of Anglican churchmanship, but it may fairly be said that his training and experience as an academic never allowed his personal sentiments to colour his work. He collected and dissected the evidence about the bones in the crypt with a dispassionate eye, and it was not until the very end of his investigation that he revealed his personal conclusion about their identity. Mason revealed his findings in a lengthy book, *What Became of the Bones of St Thomas?*, published in 1920.[3] It was by far the most comprehensive and authoritative analysis that had yet been made of the evidence and it was to take the debate into dramatically new territory.

Most of Mason's book was taken up with straightforward documentation rather than

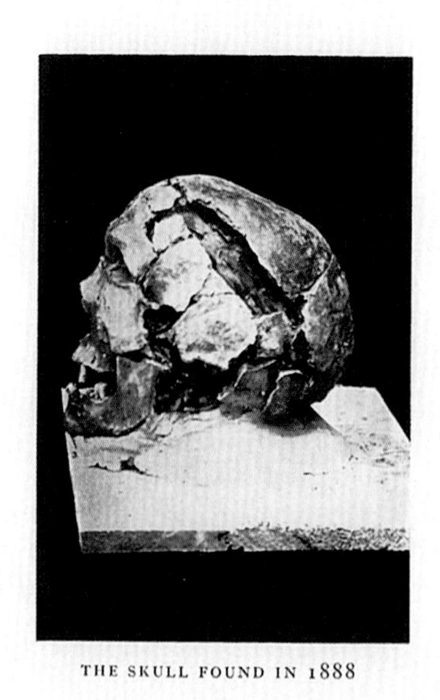

THE SKULL FOUND IN 1888

What became of the Bones of St Thomas?

A CONTRIBUTION TO HIS FIFTEENTH JUBILEE

BY

ARTHUR JAMES MASON, D.D.

CANON OF CANTERBURY

CAMBRIDGE
AT THE UNIVERSITY PRESS
1920

LEFT: Title page of Arthur Mason's book *What Became of the Bones of St Thomas*, published in 1920.

commentary or analysis. The first and most important part comprised the contemporary accounts of Becket's murder in December 1170 given by five men who had been present with the archbishop in his last hours: William of Canterbury, William fitzStephen, Benedict of Peterborough, John of Salisbury and Edward Grim. Mason regarded these accounts as important in recording the pattern of blows from the knights' swords that had landed on Becket's head and shoulders, for they allowed some sort of judgement to be made about their compatibility with the damage that Dr Pugin Thornton had observed in the skull discovered in the crypt. Unsurprisingly, Mason found many inconsistencies between the five accounts, but he nevertheless felt able, with some degree of confidence, to conclude that Becket had probably fallen onto his right side, suggesting that the vital blow which felled him would have landed on the left side of his head – consistent with Thornton's account of the large wound that he had found on that side of the skull.

Mason next reviewed the evidence on the history of Becket's bones from his murder in 1170 until the destruction of his shrine on the orders of Henry VIII. He paid particular attention to the extensive documentation that existed about the translation of the bones from the tomb in the crypt to the shrine in the Trinity Chapel in July 1220, and also to contemporary accounts of the shrine's eventual demolition in September 1538. In the last section of his book, Mason reviewed the evidence about the discovery of the grave in the eastern crypt in 1888 and the subsequent treatment of its contents. In doing so he had access to all the records that were held by the dean and chapter, and he tracked down most of the written contributions to the debate that had been made between 1888 and the time he was writing. What Mason was *not* able to do, of course, was to seek a second opinion about the bones themselves: he, like everyone else who had had their say over the years, was forced to rely on Dr Thornton's conclusions and the few photographs

ABOVE: Canon Arthur James Mason.

LEFT: Father Arthur Tooth caricatured by Spy (Leslie Ward).

of the bones that had been taken before their reinterment in February 1888.

It was not until the final few pages of his book that Canon Mason allowed himself to speculate about the identity of the person whose skeleton it might have been. The bones discovered in 1888 were, he noted, those of a man corresponding in age and height to Thomas Becket. They were the bones of one who appeared to have been killed by a blow to the left side of the head from a sharp-edged weapon. They had been removed from elsewhere to a makeshift coffin in the eastern crypt and arranged in a way that was deeply suggestive of the original disposition of Becket's bones in the shrine. Unless they were known to be the bones of someone of importance they would not have been moved to a place in the crypt that was so closely associated with Becket. There was, moreover, no direct evidence that the contents of Becket's shrine had been burned in 1538: indeed, a number of contemporary documents existed that suggested exactly the reverse.[4] 'These facts', Arthur Mason concluded, 'seem to point to the conclusion that the bones in question *are* the bones of the great Archbishop' (emphasis added).[5]

ABOVE: Plywood mock-up of Ninian Comper's design for a new shrine in the Trinity Chapel, 1930.

The clarity and authority of Mason's conclusion emboldened a number of eminent Anglo-Catholics in the Church of England to press for a fitting recognition of this glittering new jewel in Canterbury's crown. Among them were Viscount Halifax, president of the English Church Union; the Very Reverend William Hutton, dean of Winchester; Sir Samuel Hoare, who was to serve as both foreign secretary and home secretary in the 1930s; and a maverick priest, Father Arthur Tooth.[6] Though less well known than the others, Tooth was a celebrated figure in Anglo-Catholic circles because of his imprisonment in 1877 for breaches of the Public Worship Regulation Act of 1874.[7] His 'crime' had been the introduction of ritualistic practices while working as a vicar in south-east London, among them the use of incense, vestments and altar candles. Although his conviction was eventually quashed on a technicality, he became one of a small but prominent group of Anglican clergymen who were hailed by some in the Church of England as martyrs for their beliefs. It did the church no good at all.

Following the publication of Mason's book, Father Tooth began to orchestrate an audacious attempt to reconstruct the shrine of St Thomas Becket in Canterbury Cathedral.[8] Together with his wealthy backers, he offered the dean and chapter £10,000 for a new shrine to be erected in the Trinity Chapel (where Becket's original shrine had stood from 1220 until its destruction in 1538) provided the gift was matched by a further £10,000 from cathedral funds. With the offer, made in 1929, came also a design for the shrine that the group had commissioned from a leading ecclesiastical architect, Mr (later Sir) Ninian Comper. The correspondence at Lambeth Palace reveals the panic that Tooth's offer caused among the Canterbury chapter. There could, of course, be no inherent objection to glorifying the site of Becket's original shrine (a viewpoint with which the Archbishop of Canterbury, Cosmo Gordon Lang, explicitly agreed), but to do so might reopen old wounds at a very sensitive time for the Church of England. A 'private and confidential' memo that was probably written by a member of the Canterbury chapter in August 1929 warned that the construction of the new shrine 'might be interpreted as the flying of a turbulent Anglo-Catholic flag and another sign of a great move forward in that direction. The moment for inviting such a controversy is inopportune in view of the Prayer Book controversy and the Lambeth Conference next year.'[9]

The chapter bought some time for itself by agreeing to the construction *in situ* of a full-sized plywood mock-up of the shrine to show its visual effect upon the eastern end of the cathedral. The mock-up was assembled in the autumn of 1930 and was exhibited in the Trinity Chapel for several weeks. A photograph that was taken of it shows that the episcopal figures on the top of the canopy covering the shrine were as high as the capitals of the surrounding pillars. It was, in other words, a very large structure, and it was this that gave the chapter an ostensible reason for declining Father Tooth's offer. In November 1930 the dean wrote to him (and also to Ninian Comper) explaining that the shrine, if erected, would dominate not only the high altar but the whole of the choir, thereby fundamentally changing the entire visual effect of that part of the cathedral when looking eastwards. It would also be expensive at a time when the cathedral had little spare money. It is clear from the correspondence in the Jenkins' papers at Lambeth Palace, however, that an equally pressing reason for pulling the plug on the proposal was the widespread controversy that would ensue if the project went ahead.

With the benefit of hindsight, the abortive attempt to recreate the shrine of St Thomas in 1930 may be seen as providential, for Canon Arthur Mason – and all the other 'believers' since 1888 – was to be proved wrong about the bones. In 1949 the dean and chapter decided to reopen not only the issue but also the grave. The findings were to change the whole course of the debate about the bones in the crypt.

---

1. *Oxford Dictionary of National Biography*, 2004, article on Baron Davidson of Lambeth.
2. *ibid*, 2004, article on Arthur James Mason.
3. A.J. Mason, *What Became of the Bones of St Thomas?*, Cambridge, 1920.
4. These documents are examined in Chapter 10.
5. Mason, *op cit*, p. 193.
6. These names are cited in a letter from the Reverend F. G. Croom to the Dean of Canterbury, 7 July 1929. Canterbury Cathedral Archives, correspondence relating to the proposed building of a shrine, 1929/30.
7. P. T. Marsh, *The Victorian Church in Decline: Archbishop Tait and the Church of England 1868–1882*, London, 1969, pp. 225–229.
8. The extensive saga of the new shrine is documented in correspondence left to Lambeth Palace by Canon Claude Jenkins. Lambeth Palace Library, Jenkins' Papers, MS 1633, ff. 25–54.
9. Memo from 'G.C.' (possibly the Reverend F. G. Croom). Canterbury Cathedral Archives, correspondence relating to the proposed building of a shrine, 1929/30.

CHAPTER 6

THE GRAVE REVISITED

The grave in the eastern crypt of Canterbury Cathedral was reopened in the late evening of Monday 18 July 1949, sixty-one years and one hundred and fifty-nine days after it had been sealed in February 1888. On this occasion there was no Miss Holland to witness the event, but some typewritten notes, presumably made by someone who was present at the time, have been preserved in the cathedral archives.[1] According to the notes, the event was witnessed by Mr Shilling and Mr Baldock, workmen from the cathedral staff whose job it was to do the heavy lifting; Canon John Shirley, the headmaster of the King's School Canterbury and a member of the cathedral chapter; the Venerable Julian Bickersteth, archdeacon of Maidstone; Professor Alexander Cave, an anatomist from St Bartholomew's Hospital Medical College in London; Dr Jack Trevor, an archaeologist from Cambridge University; Mr Reginald Tophill, the cathedral agent; Mr Harold Anderson, the cathedral architect; and Dr William Urry, the cathedral librarian. The dean, Hewlett Johnson, arrived on the scene just as the ledger slab was being lifted.

ABOVE: Canon (Frederick) John Shirley, headmaster of the King's School Canterbury and a member of the cathedral chapter.

By now the crypt was getting dark, and a makeshift lamp was rigged up at the end of a flex plugged into a nearby organ. At 8.25 the eastern end of the slab was raised and those gathered around it could glimpse the wooden container that had been placed inside the Portland stone coffin in 1888. An unpleasant smell oozed upwards from the widening hole. Iron piping was now introduced to act as rollers, and as the slab was carefully pushed clear of the grave's opening, the onlookers peered inside. The lid of the wooden container had sunk and split, and the now-famous bones of contention could be glimpsed for the first time in over sixty years.

The broken lid of the container was lifted away, and the bones were seen to be positioned much as they had been at the first opening in 1888. They were arranged at the upper end of the coffin, not in any kind of anatomical order. The skull, still on the plaster mould around which it had been reconstructed by Dr Pugin Thornton, had fallen onto its right side. It rested on the stone pillow, cracked down the middle, as described in the original report that had been made to the dean and chapter in 1888. The bottle that had been placed behind the skull was found to be smashed and the contents saturated. The writing inside it was illegible.

LEFT: **The '1888 grave' in the eastern crypt of Canterbury Cathedral that was reopened in July 1949.**

Professor Cave and Dr Trevor quickly set to work on the bones, removing them from the coffin and laying them on sheets of paper on the floor of the crypt. In a move reminiscent of the drama in 1888, a cardboard box was brought from Canon Shirley's house into which the larger bones were placed, wrapped in paper. The skull and smaller bones were put in other boxes retrieved from the cathedral library, together with the rotten wood from the inner container. The stone coffin itself, in which the bones had originally been discovered, was not removed from the ground, but its internal dimensions were measured by Dr Urry. Everyone left the crypt, now in darkness, at about 10.20 except for the workmen and Mr Anderson, who remained behind in the small circle of electric light to close the grave and tidy up.

The decision by the chapter to reopen the grave in the summer of 1949 seems, at face value, to have been out of keeping with the times, for the insatiable appetite of the Victorians for that sort of thing had long since given way to a more respectful attitude towards the dead. According to the Chapter Acts (the minutes of the chapter meetings), the decision had been taken five months earlier, at a meeting of the chapter in February 1949, when Canon Shirley was asked to consult Professor Cave and Dr Trevor as to whether 'the proper date of the bones purported to be those of St Thomas could be ascertained'.[2] Obvious questions arise. Why did the chapter suddenly want to know how old the bones were? And why then, almost three decades after Arthur Mason had concluded that they were very probably those of Becket?

There are no more than hints of an answer in the public record. Writing in *The Times* two years later in 1951, Canon John Shirley explained that the identity of the bones in the crypt had hardened almost to the point where their authenticity had become generally accepted.[3] That would not have been at all surprising, for Mason's well-publicised conclusions had been in the public domain for almost thirty years; but the dean and chapter were, according to Shirley, 'not happy in this ascription, which might well have become, by constant repetition, avowed as fact'. But what led the chapter to have doubts about Mason's conclusions? And why did they think it necessary to do something about it at that particular moment in time?

ABOVE: Messrs Seely and Paget's design for the memorial in the western crypt of Canterbury Cathedral, 1948.

RIGHT: Chapels of St Mary Magdalene and St Nicholas in the western crypt of Canterbury Cathedral showing the broken slab in the left foreground.

Canon Shirley offered no other explanation for the chapter's decision, but the real reason (which will be revealed in Chapter Eleven) had its origin in another extraordinary event in May 1948, a full year before the grave was reopened, when the chapter agreed to begin negotiations with a well-respected London firm of ecclesiastical architects, Messrs Seely and Paget, about some sort of memorial to 'mark the burial site of St Thomas of Canterbury'.[4] In June of that year Seely and Paget were commissioned to start work on a design,[5] and a letter to the dean and chapter in August 1948 spoke of their progress in creating a memorial in the crypt 'to protect the believed resting place of Becket's bones'. In October a watercolour sketch was submitted of a design to surmount 'the tomb of St Thomas of Canterbury' depicting a brass or copper inlay in the floor of the crypt surrounded by four tall candlesticks placed on pillared stands set at an angle in each corner and linked by a gilded fence at waist height.[6]

The language used in this flurry of correspondence clearly shows that by the summer of 1948, when the commission was given to Messrs Seely and Paget, the dean and chapter had accepted Arthur Mason's conclusion that the relics of Thomas Becket had survived the destruction of his shrine in 1538 and were still buried inside the cathedral. Not only that, the chapter was preparing to take the momentous step of going public by erecting a structure to mark the spot where the bones were believed to be buried. But where was that? Common sense indicates that it *must* have been the 1888 grave in the eastern crypt, suggesting that the chapter wanted some sort of

scientific confirmation of Mason's conclusions before going ahead with the project – an insurance policy, so to speak, to ensure that a terrible mistake was not about to be made. But it was *not* the 1888 grave where the chapter believed the bones to be resting and over which the memorial was intended to be constructed. If it had been, it would have made no sense for the chapter to begin negotiations with Seely and Paget in May 1948, a full year before the 1888 grave was reopened in July 1949. Rather, the memorial was intended to surmount a *different* grave that has not yet appeared in the story – still in the crypt of the cathedral, to be sure, but in its *western* part, not its eastern part.

The evidence for this wholly unexpected turn of events is apparent in the water-colour sketch of the memorial that Seely and Paget submitted for the dean and chapter's approval in October 1948. Although the sketch is impressionistic, the architecture surrounding the structure has single columns, round arches and the tunnel vaulting of a Norman building, while the eastern crypt is in the early gothic style with double columns, pointed arches and ribbed vaulting. It is impossible to locate Seely and Paget's sketch anywhere in the *eastern* crypt but very easy to place it in the slightly earlier *western* crypt which was completed a little before 1100. Nothing more specific can be deduced from the sketch itself, but a comparison with a modern photograph shows that the site was most likely to have been the northern transept of the western crypt where all the Norman features of the sketch are found in abundance.

The transept has two adjacent apsidal chapels, one dedicated to St Mary Magdalene and the other to St Nicholas. Set into the floor in front of the two apses are two unmarked grave slabs on an east-west axis. The northernmost of the two slabs takes the form of a raised carving of the cross of Canterbury, often associated with the archbishops of Canterbury and very similar to the one that covers the tomb of Archbishop Stephen Langton in St Michael's chapel. The southernmost slab is a worn and pitted stone, flush with the floor and in two parts. A modern concrete infill provides the link between the two parts, and the sealant around three of its sides, also modern, suggests that the slab has been lifted at some time in the not-too-distant past by using the long unsealed edge as a fulcrum.

The intriguing story of these two graves in the *western* crypt and why one of them was believed by the dean and chapter in 1948 to contain the bones of St Thomas must wait until later; but first the story must return to the bones that Professor Cave and Dr Trevor took from the grave in the *eastern* crypt on that darkening evening in July 1949. Where did they go and what happened to them? And why are they *not* the bones of Thomas Becket?

---

1 Canterbury Cathedral Archives, Add. MS 313.

2 Canterbury Cathedral Chapter Acts, 5 February 1949.

3 F.J. Shirley, 'Scientists' Examination of Canterbury Bones', *The Times*, 4 August 1951. See also F.J. Shirley, 'Ancient Human Bones from Canterbury Cathedral', *Archaeologia Cantiana*, LXIV, 1951, pp. 112–115.

4 Canterbury Cathedral Chapter Acts, 22 May 1948.

5 Canterbury Cathedral Chapter Acts, 4 June 1948.

6 Messrs Seely and Paget Architects, *A suggested treatment for the tomb of St Thomas of Canterbury: A proposal within the crypt of Canterbury Cathedral*, London, 1948. Canterbury Cathedral Chapter Acts, 2 October 1948.

CHAPTER 7

A SECOND OPINION

The morning after their removal from the grave in the eastern crypt, on 19 July 1949, the bones were taken by Professor Alexander Cave to his laboratory at St Bartholomew's Hospital Medical College in London where they remained under examination for almost two years. As with the recruitment of his counterpart sixty years earlier (Dr Pugin Thornton), the reason for Cave's involvement in the re-examination of the bones is not entirely clear. He must have been sounded out, or at least covertly assessed, before the Canterbury chapter took the decision in February 1949 to consult him on the matter, but he had no known connections with Canterbury. Professor Cave was, though, an acknowledged authority on mammalian morphology, physical anthropology and medical history – precisely the expertise required to fulfil the chapter's highly unusual commission to him. His formal brief was 'to determine, in the light of present-day scientific knowledge, any intrinsic evidence which might establish, or suggest, the identity of these remains as the relics of St Thomas of Canterbury'.[1]

ABOVE: Professor Alexander Cave in 1971.

Alexander Cave's report to the dean and chapter was dated 21 May 1951.[2] It was thirty-one pages long, typewritten in double spacing, with himself as the sole signatory. There were intimations by the chapter that the report would be made public,[3] but that never happened. Quite the reverse: the report and its accompanying twenty-four photographs disappeared entirely from Canterbury, and it was only the far-sighted persistence of the cathedral archivist, Dr Michael Stansfield, in tracking down the professor at his home in north London in 1993 that enabled the only known copy of it – Cave's own personal copy – to get into the public domain.[4] Had that chance attempt to contact him failed (which might well have happened, since he died a short while later) the full story of the 1888 grave might never be known.

Having got the bones to his laboratory at St Bartholomew's Medical College, Professor Cave and his colleagues found them to be in poor condition. The wet plaster mould on which Dr Thornton had mounted the pieces of the skull in 1888 had had the unfortunate effect of introducing moisture into the sealed coffin, as a result of which the decaying process of the bones had been accelerated. Many of them had been attacked by a fungal organism. Once the

ABOVE: Museum of specimens, St Bartholomew's Hospital Medical College, London.

bones had been cleaned, the complex process began of assembling them into a skeleton. The intrinsic difficulty of the task was exacerbated by the discovery that parts of the skeleton were missing, and there were many small chips and splinters of bone that could not easily be fitted into their correct anatomical positions. Eventually, however, the reconstruction was complete and the examination began.

Professor Cave turned his attention first to the skull, since this was always likely to be the critical part of the skeleton for the purpose of identification. Dr Thornton had mounted it on the plaster mould in such a way as to show a large wound on the left side, running from behind the left ear to the middle of the forehead, with clean and straight edges. This, Thornton had surmised, could have been inflicted by a heavy cutting instrument such as a double-handed sword. Cave was absolutely clear, however, that Thornton's reconstruction had been fundamentally flawed – and he had probably done it in such a way as to produce the effect that he had wanted to see. In fact, once the pieces of the skull had been reassembled correctly, they showed no evidence at all of any ante-mortem damage by a cutting instrument. There were cracks and fractures, certainly, but they had all been caused *after* death and they had not been caused instrumentally.

This fact alone decisively scuppered the belief that the bones might be those of Becket, for nobody doubted that he had suffered at least one mighty blow to his head from a sword *before* he died – the blow that very probably killed him. But there was more, for Cave also found that all the cracks and fractures in the skull had been caused by the natural shifting over time of the earth in which it must originally have been buried. In other words, the person whose skull it had once been had first been buried in bare earth, not in a coffin. The subsequent damage to the skull was a process – well known to osteo-archaeologists – called 'grave-weathering', and Cave concluded that the condition of the skeleton in his laboratory 'tallied exactly with archaeological material of Romano-British, Anglo-Saxon and XVIIIth century dates with which they have been compared.'[5] This, too, was a decisive finding, for there is no evidence that Becket's body had ever been buried in bare earth. The skull in Professor Cave's laboratory could not have been his.

Having blown asunder the hopes of Arthur Mason and all the other 'believers' since 1888, much of Professor Cave's examination of the rest of the skeleton was something of an anti-climax. He confirmed Dr Thornton's conclusion that it was a male skeleton of at least forty-five years of age, but he suggested a higher upper age limit than Thornton had proposed – sixty or even more. The man had been of robust build and about five feet eight inches in height – quite tall for an early medieval man (if that is what he was) but much less than Thornton's estimate of six feet two inches. He had probably been right-handed and had suffered from osteoarthritis in the spine. Many small bones from all parts of the skeleton were missing and only five teeth remained in the skull. At an informed guess (since carbon-14 dating was not yet widely available in the early 1950s) Cave dated the skeleton back to the medieval period, possibly the 12th century.

It was not until nearly the end of his report that Professor Cave introduced a dramatic new element into the story. In addition to the bones of the reconstructed skeleton, the coffin also contained an assortment of other bony fragments. Most of them came from domestic animals, including pigs, sheep, a small ox and a bird. There was also an incomplete upper vertebra from another, smaller human skeleton. No mention of these had been made in the original report to the dean and chapter. It had certainly been noted by the investigating committee that the coffin contained 'much earthen debris'[6] which Thornton later said he had 'carefully sifted'[7]; but he made no mention of any extraneous bones being left over after the skeleton had been reconstructed. Had the presence of these alien items been noticed and reported, and had the appropriate conclusions been drawn from them, the whole course of the debate since 1888 might have taken a fundamentally different course.

Professor Cave himself helpfully explained to the dean and chapter the significance of the additional bones: the skeleton had originally been buried in bare earth, probably in a communal burial place, and had later been exhumed, along with some of the surrounding soil containing the bone fragments of other people and animals buried nearby, before being deposited in the coffin in the eastern crypt. And there was more: not only had the skeleton been buried in a communal earthen grave, the original burial had been of a complete human corpse, not a collection of bones. The evidence for this was clear and dramatic, for after reassembling the skeleton Cave found a number of instances where anatomically contiguous bones in the pelvis, femur, patella and tibia had been damaged by spade cuts that could only have been inflicted while they were in their correct skeletal positions. What had been buried in the earth was a body; what had been exhumed were the remains of that body in which some of the bones in the pelvis and legs were still in their correct anatomical positions when they were damaged by the spades of those who had dug them up.

Cave offered one final important deduction about the history of the skeleton from his examination of it: prior to being placed in the coffin in the crypt, it had been exhumed in great haste, or with little care, or both. Indeed, the phrase that Cave chose to describe the exhumation process was 'gross and destructive carelessness'. This conclusion is of such importance in unravelling the mystery of the grave in the eastern crypt that it merits quoting Cave's words in full.

> 'The exhumation was conducted with such apparent carelessness as to create the impression that the operation was not the deliberate excavation of known human remains from a known site, but rather the accidental uncovering of a human burial during some digging operation. The deliberate search for, and excavation of, a known burial would surely have been conducted with greater care, both in the digging out of the skeleton and in the securing of all the bones. The breaking of so many of the bones and the leaving behind of so much of the skull, spine, hands and feet may indicate an accidental rather than a deliberate exhumation.'[8]

Professor Cave concluded his report to the dean and chapter by expressing the hope that he had adequately fulfilled their commission to him. It was, he confessed, a personal disappointment that he had not been able to confirm the bones as those of St Thomas Becket, but he added – quite properly – that the issue had to be resolved solely on the evidence afforded by the skeleton itself. For the first time in more than sixty years, science was now dictating the course of this curious tale. But it still had a long way to go.

---

1 Letter to the Dean and Chapter of Canterbury Cathedral from Professor A.J.E. Cave accompanying the submission of his report, May 1951, Canterbury Cathedral Library.

2 A.J.E. Cave, *Report to the Dean and Chapter of Canterbury Cathedral on a Skeleton Buried in the Cathedral Crypt*, unpublished MS, May 1951, Canterbury Cathedral Library.

3 Canterbury Cathedral Chapter Acts, 22 September 1951.

4 Professor Cave had not kept any of the photographs, which seem to have disappeared completely.

5 Cave, *op cit*, p. 9.

6 C.F. Routledge, J.B. Sheppard and W.A. Scott Robertson, 'The Crypt of Canterbury Cathedral', *Archaeologia Cantiana*, XVIII, 1889, p. 256.

7 W.P. Thornton, *What Became of the Bones of St Thomas?*, Canterbury, 1901, p. 3.

8 Cave, *op cit*, p. 30.

CHAPTER 8

DECOY!

The bones came back to Canterbury from Professor Cave's laboratory in London in June 1951, just as the Festival of Britain was getting into its stride. They were placed inside a lead box and buried, for at least the third time in their existence, in the Portland stone coffin that had remained in the grave in the eastern crypt. The little ceremony was conducted by Canon John Shirley. The grave was then sealed with a plain, unmarked slab set flush with the level of the floor.[1] Yet this was by no means the end of the story, for although the bones had been returned to their historic resting place, even more questions had now been raised about them. If the bones in the 1888 grave were *not* Becket's, whose were they? And how did they come to be there? What sequence of events could possibly have led to the remains of an unknown and apparently insignificant man being carelessly dug up from a communal burial site and hastily interred in a revered location in the bowels of Canterbury Cathedral? Trying to answer these questions seemed rather like doing a jigsaw puzzle without a picture whilst knowing that important pieces were missing. Yet thanks to Professor Cave and his team, some very significant pieces in the puzzle *were* now to hand, and it may be helpful to summarise them before the narrative lurches on.

ABOVE: Logo for the Festival of Britain, 1951.

An unknown man, possibly living in the early middle ages, was buried in an earthen grave in a common burial site where other bones, including those of domestic animals, were also to be found. The site may have been next to, or used by, a butchery or slaughterhouse. The man was of late middle age, fairly tall for his time, and had suffered from osteoarthritis in his spine. He had probably died a natural death since there was no evidence of any instrumental trauma to his skeleton other than the marks inflicted by the spade(s) that later dug him up. Since he had been buried without a coffin in a common burial place, he is unlikely to have been a man of any social standing.

Then, at a later but unknown date, the man's body, now reduced to a skeleton, was exhumed from its earthen grave in a hasty and careless manner, inflicting spade cuts on several of the bones in the pelvis and legs and leaving some smaller bones behind. Together with a quantity of the surrounding soil, which contained fragments of animal and other human bones, the exhumed skeleton was taken into the eastern crypt of Canterbury Cathedral where it was buried in line with, and only a few feet away from, the place where St Thomas Becket had first been interred following his murder in December 1170.

The bones were placed in a small stone coffer, too small to take a complete human body, with the skull raised up on a stone cushion and the long bones arranged around it. As far as is known, this ritualistic disposition of the bones replicated the way in which Becket's relics had been laid out in his shrine in the Trinity Chapel when they were placed there in July 1220. The coffer was then buried in a very shallow grave, only a few inches beneath the level of the crypt floor, where it appears to have remained undisturbed until its accidental discovery on 23 January 1888.

These are the hard facts. Their sources have been cited and can be checked by anyone who wishes to do so. It is, of course, possible that Professor Cave was wrong in some of his findings, but his report was accepted in its entirety by the dean and chapter in 1951 (as Canon John Shirley's article in *The Times* in 1951 made clear)[2], and his conclusions have not been challenged since they first became public in 1993. So what is to be made of this extremely puzzling sequence of events? Hardly any plausible theories can be posited that take account of *all* the known facts. A number of elaborate explanations have been suggested, but they are so full of subterfuge and skulduggery that they founder on the rocks of improbability. Others carry conviction only by conveniently ignoring some of the evidence. Only one theory has emerged so far that is both plausible *and* faithful to the evidence – that the grave was deliberately created as a decoy to deceive the commissioners of King Henry VIII when they arrived in Canterbury in September 1538 to destroy the shrine of St Thomas. A possible sequence of events can be imagined.

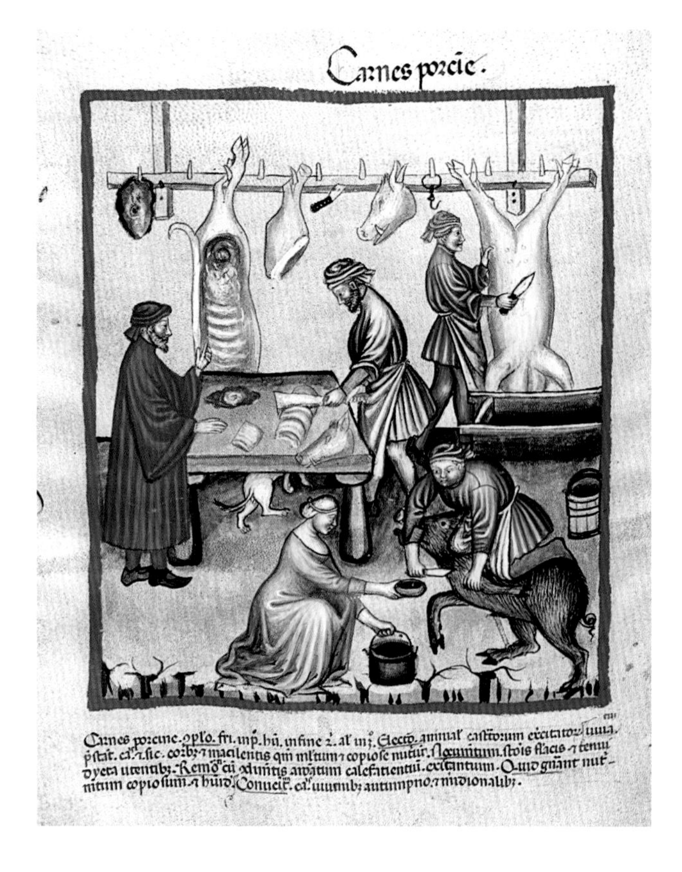

ABOVE: A medieval slaughterhouse.

RIGHT: Burial of Thomas Becket in the crypt of Canterbury Cathedral, from an English psalter of c. 1200.

Knowing what had happened in other monastic settings, and willing to do anything to protect their sacred treasure, the monks of the cathedral removed Becket's true relics from the shrine, hid them in a secret place, and replaced them with substitutes to await discovery and disposal by the king's commissioners. The monks would have known of similar deceptions rumoured to have been carried out by their Benedictine brethren elsewhere, and this – in spite of the manifest and serious risks – could have emboldened them to do the same at Canterbury. Then, to guard against the possibility that the deception would be discovered and a search made for the place where the real relics had been secreted, the monks deliberately created a decoy grave containing bones for the commissioners to find and despoil. To do its job, the grave would have to be in a fairly obvious place and it would have to give all the appearance of having been hastily prepared to take the true relics. A shallow burial in the crypt immediately adjacent to Becket's first place of burial would satisfy these twin requirements.

To carry out their plan, the monks would have needed to acquire a set of bones, presumably in a clandestine way that would not have drawn attention to what they were doing. A night-time raid on a communal burial site where human bodies and animal carcasses were flung together in bare earth might well have offered the best chance of obtaining what they needed. Once there, the grave robbers would have had to act swiftly in the darkness, digging up the first skeleton they encountered with little heed for any damage they may be inflicting on it. Needing to work quickly, they would not have had sufficient time to ensure that all the bones were gathered in, and in their rushed attempt to get as much of the skeleton as possible, a quantity of the surrounding earth was scooped up with the bones and taken into the cathedral.

Once in the safety of the crypt, a shallow grave was dug. A deeper grave would have been self-defeating, since the commissioners would have realised that the monks might not have had the time to do so. In any case, it was crucial to the deception that the decoy grave, if called into

BELOW: Site of St Cuthbert's shrine, Durham Cathedral.

action, should be found without too much searching. Using whatever suitable receptacle was to hand, the monks then arranged the bones in the way that Becket's relics had been laid out in the shrine, giving particular prominence to the skull by raising it up on a stone cushion. It is likely that all the bones from the burial site were placed in the coffer, for the monks would not have known that some of them had actually come from animals. Thus hastily prepared, the decoy coffer and its fake contents were lowered into the shallow grave to await its possible discovery.

This conjectured sequence of events may be wrong and it may eventually be shown to be so. It contains a number of obvious difficulties. Yet it does account for all the known facts, and it behoves those who believe it to be wrong to posit a better one. To reject the decoy theory simply because it raises politically awkward questions, or even that it is just plain fanciful, will not do. Whether wanted or not, the grave and its enigmatic contents are there in the eastern crypt of Canterbury cathedral and they cannot be wished away. There *must* be an explanation of how they came to be there, and it is entirely reasonable to wonder what it might be. The decoy theory may not be correct, but it is true to the evidence; and whilst it may properly be challenged, it would be pointless to do so without proposing an alternative that takes equal account of what is now known about the 1888 grave and its enigmatic contents.

It follows from the decoy theory that the monks of Canterbury Cathedral had at least *tried* to protect the precious relics of St Thomas from the destructive intentions of the king's commissioners. Whether they succeeded is an entirely different matter; but it is possible that they were not alone in *attempting* to safeguard their sacred treasure, for there is evidence that others may have been doing similar things elsewhere. The case of the great northern saint, Cuthbert, is perhaps the closest parallel to Becket's and also the best documented.[3]

St Cuthbert's shrine in Durham cathedral was destroyed by Henry VIII's commissioners in the winter of 1539 – a year after Becket's at Canterbury. His relics were removed and placed in the cathedral revestry where they remained for two years before being buried in a grave that was dug beneath the place where the shrine had stood. There is no evidence that any bones were destroyed.[4] The grave was opened in May 1827 in a ramshackle and probably unauthorised excavation undertaken by the canon librarian, the Reverend James Raine. The documentation that exists from the time gives a confused account of exactly what was found, but it seems clear that three coffins were discovered in the grave, stacked one upon another. The first two coffins contained a large assortment of bones, from both adults and children, while the third contained a complete human skeleton 'swathed in shrouds of linen or silk'.[5] Though totally unqualified to do so, Raine himself conducted an examination of the skeleton before concluding to his own satisfaction that it was indeed that of St Cuthbert. Raine then reburied it in a flimsy packing case that soon disintegrated.

The grave was opened again in March 1899 and the skeleton in the rotting packing case was removed for examination, this time by a 'competent anatomist'[6] (who, unlike his counterpart Dr Pugin Thornton at Canterbury, was not named). The results were equivocal. The anatomist found enough evidence to conclude that the skeleton could have been that of the saint, but much of it was circumstantial (to do with height, age, and the shape of the skull) and there were no signs of the serious diseases from which Cuthbert was said to have suffered in his lifetime and which would have been detectable in any competent examination of the skeleton (including 'an acrid tumour of the knee, the bubo [inflammation of a lymph node] in the groin, the callosity at the junction of foot and leg, and the ulcer of the foot').[7]

Although many at the time clearly believed the skeleton to be that of St Cuthbert, an alternative explanation was offered by Father William Brown, a local Roman Catholic priest who had been invited to take part in the 1899 investigation. He drew attention to a long-standing tradition that at some time after 1539, while the saint's relics were still in the revestry of Durham Cathedral awaiting King Henry's decision about their eventual fate, they were 'spirited away' and hidden in a secret part of the cathedral to prevent their desecration.[8] Then, in order to deceive the commissioners if the king eventually decided to destroy the relics, a substitute skeleton was taken from a local graveyard and left in its place in the revestry. As things turned out, no such destruction was ordered, and what was buried in the new grave beneath the shrine was the decoy skeleton, not the genuine relics. The tradition that the true relics remained in a safe place elsewhere in the cathedral was invoked by Sir Walter Scott in his celebrated narrative poem *Marmion*, adding the conspiratorial detail that the secret had been known only by three monks (who had presumably organised the deception).

> 'There deep in Durham's Gothic shade
> His [Cuthbert's] relics are in secret laid,
> But none may know the place
> Save of his holiest servants three
> Who share that wondrous grace.'

Before leaving the grave in the eastern crypt of Canterbury Cathedral, the obvious point must be made that, as far as the evidence shows, it was never found: it seems to have been discovered in 1888 exactly as it had been left at, or just before, the destruction of Becket's shrine in 1538. If this is true, one of two things could have happened: either the commissioners discovered the true relics and therefore had no need to search elsewhere, or they discovered what they *thought* were the true relics, and again had no need to search in other places. If the former was the case, the debate about the fate of Becket's bones is at an end: the monks' deception failed and the true relics were disposed of. If the latter was the case, then the monks' deception succeeded and the relics somehow survived. But could that have been possible? It is to this question that the investigation must now turn.

---

1 Canterbury Cathedral Chapter Acts, 23 June 1951.

2 F.J. Shirley, 'Scientists' Examination of Canterbury Bones', *The Times*, 4 August 1951. See also F.J. Shirley, 'Ancient Human Bones from Canterbury Cathedral', *Archaeologia Cantiana*, LXIV, 1951, pp. 112–115.

3 The tortuous story of St Cuthbert's relics is told in D. Willem, *St Cuthbert's Corpse: A Life After Death*, Durham, 2013. The story is complicated by the fact that the primary objective of the two excavations in 1827 and 1899 was not just the identification of the relics but the testing of the long-held belief that Cuthbert's body had survived intact and uncorrupted since his death in the mid-630s.

4 *ibid*, p. 57.

5 *ibid*, p. 67.

6 *ibid*, p. 84.

7 *ibid*, p. 88.

8 *ibid*, pp. 86, 90.

CHAPTER 9

COULD THE BONES OF ST THOMAS BECKET HAVE SURVIVED?

If the monks of Canterbury Cathedral *had* tried to deceive King Henry VIII's commissioners, as the theory of the decoy grave implies, did they succeed? Could the relics of St Thomas Becket have survived the destruction of his shrine? There is no definitive answer, for no authentic record has come to light of the events that took place in the cathedral in September 1538; but evidence can be found to support both sides of the argument.

As the national debate that followed the discovery of the grave in the eastern crypt in 1888 showed, there was no shortage of circumstantial evidence to justify the claim that nothing could have survived from the destruction of Becket's shrine (Chapter Four). Much of this evidence was contextual: doubters pointed out, for example, that had the relics survived, they would have been reinstated during the reign of Queen Mary Tudor between 1553 and 1558. Others found it impossible to believe that the monks would have risked life and limb by attempting to deceive the commissioners when the king himself was so deeply hostile to the cult of St Thomas.

ABOVE: Queen Mary Tudor (Mary I), by Master John.

To these perfectly reasonable arguments there were, of course, perfectly reasonable rejoinders. Historians pointed out that even in places where saintly relics were known to have survived, their shrines were never reinstated during the Marian period. English Catholicism had moved on, and enthusiasm for the cult of the saints had been waning for some time – not least in Canterbury where pilgrim numbers arriving at the cathedral had been at an historically low ebb for more than a hundred years. Few wanted to see a return to former Catholic practices like the cult of the saints and the worship of relics.

As for the risks that the monks of the cathedral may have been running in trying to conceal the bones, it was argued that the remains of their beloved saint would have been of such supreme importance to them that they would have been prepared to risk even their lives to prevent a sacrilegious bonfire. After all, they would only have been following the example of the martyred archbishop himself, who had given his life in defence of the church.

More telling than these contextual arguments for and against the destruction of the relics were the claims circulating at the time that the bones of St Thomas had been burnt, probably in the cathedral itself and possibly even in the presence of King Henry's chief minister, Thomas Cromwell. The rumours about the burning originated on the mainland of Europe where Catholic opinion was outraged by reports about the king's actions at Canterbury. At a consistory in Rome

LEFT: Pope Paul III, by Titian.

on 25 October 1538 (about six weeks after the destruction of Becket's shrine) Pope Paul III 'announced the new cruelty and impiety of the King of England, who had commanded the body of St Thomas of Canterbury to be burnt and the ashes scattered to the wind'.[1] Significantly, the pope's accusation was not that the relics had *actually* been burnt, only that Henry had *ordered* it to be done. Two months later, in a papal bull of excommunication against the king in December 1538, the pope again accused Henry of ordering the burning of the bones, but again no mention was made of any actual burning: 'He [the king] has commanded those bones to be exhumed and burned, and the ashes scattered to the wind.'[2] Yet once the pope had implied that the burning had indeed occurred, few were likely to challenge him by questioning the distinction between the command and the deed. Becket's bones *had* been burnt.

At about the same time, communications from English ambassadors in Europe were reporting an interest on the continent in the fate of the saint's relics.[3] People were asking what had become of them. Following the lead given by Pope Paul III, the answer was commonly proffered that they had been consumed by fire. The story even reached the ears of Cardinal Reginald Pole in Rome

ABOVE: **Cardinal Reginald Pole, by Sebastiano del Piombo.**

(later to become Archbishop of Canterbury under Mary Tudor) who complained to the Emperor Charles V about Henry's 'ungodliness' and 'barbarity'.[4]

In time, the accusations of Pope Paul and Cardinal Pole came to be repeated in a number of other Catholic publications. They included works by Thomas Stapleton, a prebendary of Chichester under Mary Tudor and one of the most learned Catholics of his day, and by Nicholas Sanders, a Catholic theologian who later took refuge on the continent and wrote a critique of the religious life of England under Queen Elizabeth.[5] Further testimony to the burning was given by Nicander Nucius, a Greek traveller who attached himself to a German ambassadorial party that was passing through Canterbury in 1545 on its way to London. Whilst in the city, Nucius claimed to have picked up several pieces of recent news, including the destruction of St Thomas's shrine and the burning of his bones in the streets of Canterbury after they had been dragged 'along the public road and exposed to the gaze of the populace'. Then, 'having put the ashes into a cannon, they were discharged into the air'.[6]

The story of the burning gained ground in England through the writings of the 16th-century chroniclers, especially Charles Wriothesley, John Stow and the compilers of the Holinshed Chronicles. None of these was actually present when the shrine was destroyed, and their hearsay accounts bear several similarities to each other, suggesting that they may have drawn their material from a common source. Wriothesley's narrative is particularly interesting.[7] He contradicted Nicander Nucius by stating that the bones of St Thomas were 'brent' (burnt) inside the cathedral, not in the streets of the city, adding that the deed was done in the presence of 'my Lord Crumwell'. Wriothesley continued by noting that among the objects removed from the shrine was the saint's skull, complete with the wounds of his martyrdom.[8] If true, this observation is highly significant, for something that purported to be Becket's skull, enclosed in a silver reliquary, had long been shown to pilgrims visiting Canterbury Cathedral. With the removal of the relics from the shrine, 'skull and all', the deceit that had been perpetrated by the monks for generations became openly known.

A difficulty common to all the claims about the burning of bones is the absence not only of any eye-witness accounts of the event but also of any certainty about whose bones – if anyone's – were consigned to the flames. Even if bones *had* been burnt in the cathedral or in the streets of the city, it cannot automatically be assumed that they were Becket's. If, for example, the monks had succeeded in introducing substitute bones for the commissioners to find and burn, then nobody other than those who were party to the deception would have known what was really going up in flames – and they were obviously not going to say. In any case, there were plenty of other relics in the cathedral that could have been burnt as a convenient way of getting rid of them.

There is, moreover, an important contemporary voice that seems to speak against the destruction of St Thomas's relics. Writing to Thomas Cromwell on 27 September 1538,

Thomas Wriothesley, the Earl of Southampton and a cousin of the chronicler Charles, reported a conversation he had had about the treatment of relics with Stephen Gardiner, the Bishop of Winchester. Wriothesley told Cromwell that Gardiner, who had just passed through Canterbury on his way home from Europe and would therefore have heard at first hand exactly what had happened, 'did not seem to dislike the doing at Canterbury … and wished the like were done at Winchester'.[9] Gardiner had been a resolute opponent of the new doctrines of the Reformation and he was anxious to ensure that England did not abandon the traditional faith.[10] For his pains, he was imprisoned in the Tower of London by Edward VI; but upon Mary Tudor's accession to the throne in 1553 he was released in time to crown her as queen in the chapel of Whitehall Palace. In the following year Gardiner conducted Mary's marriage to Philip of Spain in Winchester Cathedral.

OPPOSITE: Bishop Stephen Gardiner, by Quentin Massys.

ABOVE: Thomas Cromwell, by Hans Holbein the Younger.

It seems highly unlikely that such a strong Catholic traditionalist as Bishop Stephen Gardiner would reportedly have said that he 'did not dislike the doing at Canterbury' if he knew that the relics of St Thomas had been burnt or otherwise despoiled. More than that, he expressed the hope that whatever had been done to Becket's relics at Canterbury had also been done to those of St Swithun in Winchester Cathedral. Gardiner's conversation with Wriothesley must have taken place very soon after the destruction of Swithun's shrine on 25 September 1538, but being abroad at the time he had not yet learnt what had happened to the relics. He clearly hoped, however, that they had been treated in the same way as Becket's. Having heard at first-hand what had been done at Canterbury, Gardiner's testimony strongly implies that nothing of a sacrilegious nature was perpetrated there. It is known that saintly relics were sometimes buried discreetly in out-of-the-way places where they would no longer be a focus of pious veneration, and this could well have been the disposal method that Gardiner approved of for St Thomas.

Yet Stephen Gardiner's comments are not without their difficulties, for they do not sit easily with the possibility, implicit in the decoy theory, that the monks had attempted to deceive the king's commissioners by removing the true relics of St Thomas from his shrine and replacing them with other bones to be found and dealt with (Chapter Eight). If this had indeed been the case, then it would have been the treatment of the substitute relics, not the true ones, that elicited Gardiner's approval. He would have been as much a victim of the monks' deception as the commissioners themselves. Even in this eventuality, however, the central fact would remain that Gardiner 'did not dislike' the commissioners' treatment of relics that he *believed* to be the true ones. They were disposed of in an acceptable manner.

To the 16th-century voice of Bishop Stephen Gardiner may be added weighty 20th-century voices that also incline towards the survival rather than the destruction of Becket's relics in

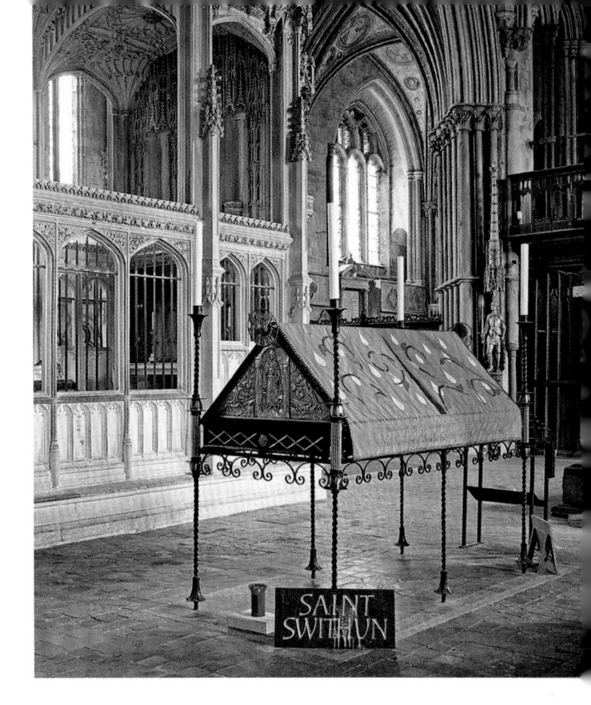

ABOVE: Site of St Swithun's shrine, Winchester Cathedral.

1538. The first is that of Canon Arthur Mason, who was commissioned by the Archbishop of Canterbury, Randall Davidson, to review the accumulated evidence to date about the grave in the eastern crypt (Chapter Five). In his book *What Became of the Bones of St Thomas?*, published in 1920, Mason concluded that the evidence pointed towards the bones in the 1888 grave as those of Thomas Becket.[11] He was later shown by Professor Alexander Cave to have been wrong about this, but having carefully reviewed the extant material about the events of 1538 Mason thought it more likely than not that the relics had survived – otherwise he would not have reached the conclusion he did.

Canon Mason's voice must be accorded due weight. So too must the voices of the members of the Canterbury Cathedral chapter in 1948 when they commissioned Messrs Seely and Paget to design a memorial 'to protect the believed resting place of Becket's bones' (Chapter Six).[12] That decision, which is dissected in Chapter Eleven, would have made no sense unless the members of the chapter had accepted the survival of the relics. Indeed, the minutes of the chapter's decision explicitly declared this to be the case by referring to 'the believed resting place of Becket's bones'. This position, too, must be accorded due weight.

Where does this leave us? The evidence is inconclusive. Bones may have been burnt in September 1538, either in Canterbury Cathedral (Charles Wriothesley) or in the streets of the city (Nicander Nucius), but if so, there is no direct evidence that they were the relics of St Thomas. The story of the burning originated with Pope Paul III in Rome in October 1538 and was quickly taken up by Catholic churchmen and polemicists as well as by European ambassadors and English chroniclers; but Pope Paul, who excommunicated Henry VIII in December 1538 for his alleged part in the sacrilegious bonfire, apparently knew no more than that the king had ordered it. If the Vatican had any evidence that the burning had actually taken place, it has not come into the public domain. The reported reaction of the traditionalist Bishop Stephen Gardiner in the aftermath of the shrine's destruction in 1538, together with the conclusions of Canon Arthur Mason in 1920 and of the Canterbury chapter in 1948, add further weight to the possibility that the relics *could* have survived. However, some rather more direct contemporary information has survived in the records compiled by two clerks of the Privy Council in about 1539 and 1552, and it is to this that the investigation must now turn.

---

1 J. Gairdner (ed), *Letters and Papers, Foreign and Domestic, on the Reign of Henry VIII*, London, 1893, XIII, pt. II, 684.
2 *ibid*, XIII, pt. II, 1087.
3 *ibid*, XIII, pt. II, 542, 684.
4 *ibid*, XIV, pt. I, 200, 536.
5 G. Constant, *The Reformation in England: 1 The English Schism*, London, 1934, pp. 443 and 453–454.
6 J.A. Cramer (tr.), *The Second Book of the Travels of Nicander Nucius of Corcyra*, London (Camden Society), 1841, pp. 74–75.
7 W.D. Hamilton (ed), *A Chronicle of England During the Reigns of the Tudors from AD 1485 to 1559 by Charles Wriothesley, Windsor Herald*, London (Camden Society), 1875, p. 86.
8 *ibid*, pp. 86–87.
9 Gairdner, *op cit*, XIII, pt. II, 442.
10 *Oxford Dictionary of National Biography*, 2004, article on Bishop Stephen Gardiner.
11 A.J. Mason, *What Became of the Bones of St Thomas?*, Cambridge, 1920, p. 193.
12 Canterbury Cathedral Chapter Acts, 22 May 1948 and 4 June 1948.

CHAPTER 10

TWO CLERKS OF THE PRIVY COUNCIL

Although there are second-hand reports that bones were burnt either in Canterbury Cathedral or in the city following the dismantling of St Thomas's shrine in September 1538, there is no direct evidence that they were those of the saint. They could just as well have been some of the many bony relics that were littering the cathedral on the eve of the Reformation and that aroused the distaste of Erasmus when he visited Canterbury a few years earlier in 1512.[1] When to this is added the possibility that the monks of the cathedral took active steps to protect their precious treasure from the destructive purposes of King Henry VIII by creating a decoy grave for the commissioners to find and if necessary despoil, it is reasonable to conclude that Becket's relics *could* have survived the destruction of his shrine and been buried elsewhere for safe keeping. Records left by two 16th-century clerks of the Privy Council, Thomas Derby and William Thomas, suggest just that; but like so much else in this labyrinthine tale, their words are indicative rather than conclusive.

The first record occurs in an official statement that was probably drawn up at the beginning of 1539. Issued by the Paper Office, it is titled *Official Account of the Reformation: Vindication of the Changes Recently Effected in England.*[2] The original version, now in the National Archives, is in the handwriting of Thomas Derby, a man of learning who had the confidence of Thomas Cromwell and who was appointed to the Privy Council in March 1538.[3] He became its clerk in the following year. The statement may have been intended as a sermon to be preached from St Paul's Cross, as some have suggested,[4] or it may simply have been prepared for use on the continent by ambassadors and agents who wished – or had been instructed – to promote King Henry's point of view. Whatever its intended use, the statement seems to be some sort of official reply by the Privy Council to the charges that originated in Rome in October 1538 about the burning of relics (Chapter Nine).

The reference to Becket's shrine begins: 'As for the shryne of Thomas Becket ...' and it continues with a reconstructed history of Becket's crimes against the royal prerogative. There then appears the following sentence:

ABOVE: Preaching at Old St Paul's Cross.

LEFT: A Tudor council in session.

'His [Becket's] shryne and bones shuld be taken away and bestowed in suche place as the same shuld cause no superstition afterwards, as it is indede amongst others of that sorte conveyed and buryed in a noble towre.'

For whatever reason, the second half of the sentence has been crossed through in the original. In his book *What Became of the Bones of St Thomas?*, Canon Arthur Mason expressed the view that the 'noble towre' in question was very probably the Tower of London.[5] In the case of St Richard, for example, the commission for the destruction of his shrine in Chichester Cathedral required any of his relics, including his bones, to be taken to the Tower along with the remains of the shrine itself;[6] and Mason surmised that Thomas Derby had initially made the same assumption about Becket in the Privy Council's document. But why, then, was the second part of the sentence, including the phrase about the 'noble towre', subsequently crossed out? Could it be, Mason wondered, that someone had made the deletion when it later became apparent that something else had happened to the relics – that they had not, after all, been taken to the Tower along with the shrine and the jewels?

The text of the Privy Council's statement did not end there, however: it continued by affirming the accounts of Charles Wriothesley and the other English chroniclers that a skull which had been presented to pilgrims for generations as that of St Thomas was actually a fake (Chapter Nine).

'And for as moche as his [Becket's] hedd almost hole was found with the rest of his bones closed within the shryne, and that ther was in that church a grete scull of another hede ... *whereby it appered that the same was but a feyned fiction* ...' (emphasis added).

Here, Thomas Derby affirms that the real head of Becket, almost complete, was taken from the shrine along with the rest of the bones, and the 'grete scull of another hede' was thus exposed as a deception. This other skull, that generations of pilgrims had been invited to kiss in the belief that it was truly Becket's, was no more than 'a feyned fiction'. The reason for the Privy Council's exposure of the deceit is not hard to imagine: King Henry would have relished making a public example of the monks' duplicity at a time when he was about to close their monastery (which happened in the following year, 1540).

There was more. The next part of the sentence added a critically important observation:

'... if this hede [the 'grete scull of another hede'] was brent, was therfore St Thomas brent? Assurydly, it concludeth not.'

At first sight, these words in the Privy Council's statement appear to affirm that, although a skull was burnt, it was not the one that had been taken from the shrine. It was not, in other words, Becket's true skull that was burnt but the 'feyned fiction'. Yet the text does not quite allow this interpretation: the fact that a counterfeit skull was burnt is not itself conclusive evidence that the true skull was not also burnt. It is as though Thomas Derby wished to create the impression that the true relic had escaped the flames but could not quite bring himself to say so directly.

The next sentence in the Privy Council's statement suggests that a similar sequence of events may have occurred at Winchester Cathedral, where the relics of St Swithun were removed from their shrine in the retrochoir on 25 September 1538 – a few days later than Becket's at Canterbury.

'St Swythan and other reliques, whereaboute abuse of ipocrasy was, be layde safe, and not, as it is untruely surmitted, brent, but according to reason collocate secretely, wher ther shal be no cause of superstition giuen to them, as some say that for the like cause the body of Moyses was hyden lest the Jues shuld fall to idolatory.'

As at Canterbury, allegations were made that an 'abuse of ipocrasy' had been perpetrated by the monks of Winchester against the relics of St Swithun, and rumours had arisen in the aftermath of the shrine's destruction that they had been burnt. But according to Thomas Derby's record, those rumours were untrue: far from being burnt, Swithun's relics had been secreted away to prevent them from becoming objects of idolatrous worship. They were, in Derby's words, 'layde safe'. It has already been noted that the Bishop of Winchester at the time, Stephen Gardiner, had first-hand knowledge of the fate of Becket's bones at Canterbury and hoped that

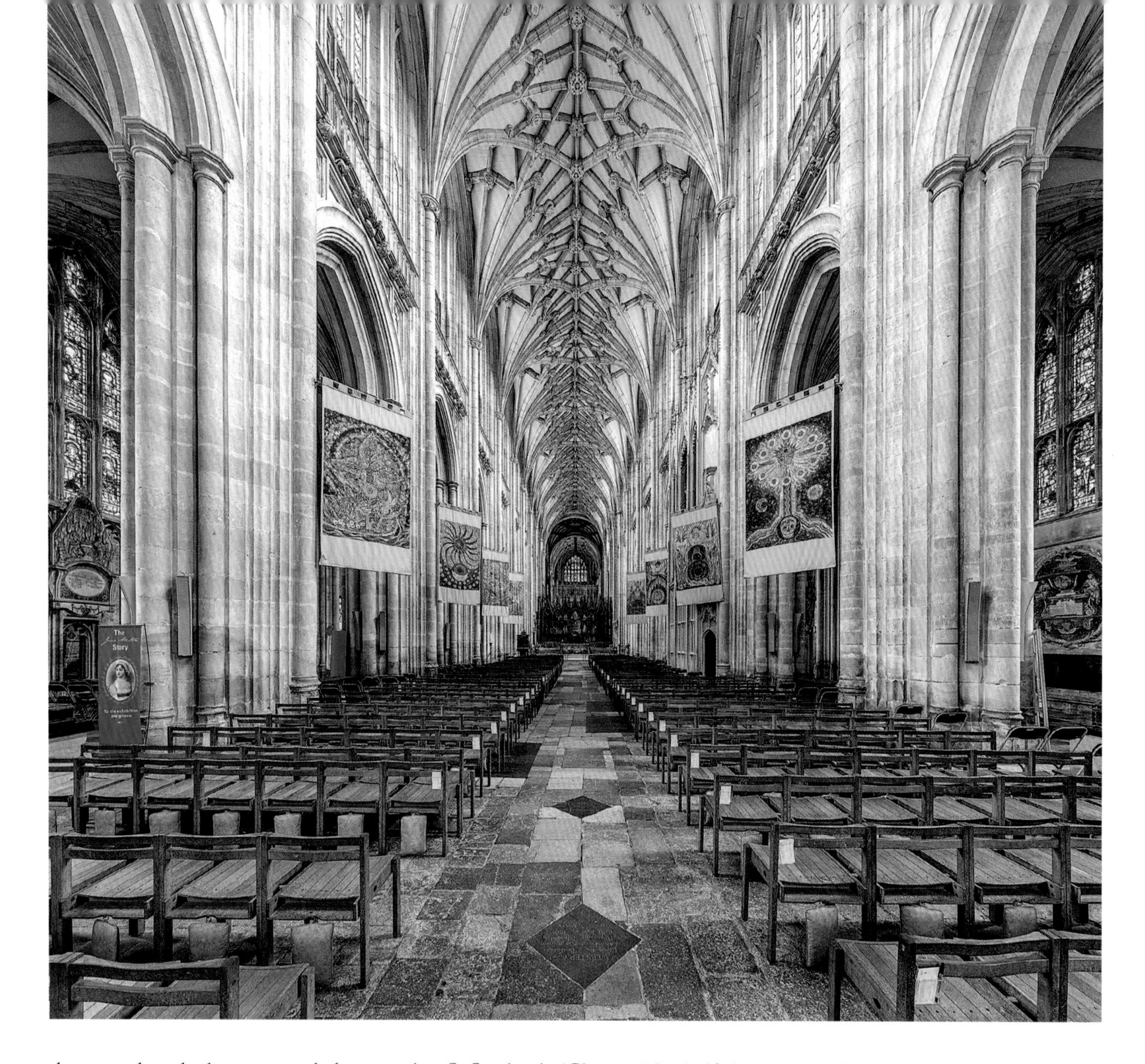

ABOVE: Winchester Cathedral.

the same thing had very recently happened to St Swithun's (Chapter Nine). If the actions taken at Winchester had indeed been the same as those at Canterbury, as Gardiner hoped, then the relics of both Becket and Swithun *could* have survived the destruction of their shrines and been secreted away in safe places, probably within their respective cathedrals. Contemporary opinion in Winchester accepts that Swithun's relics may still lie buried in an unmarked grave somewhere within the cathedral or its precincts.[7]

A further defence against the charge of the burning of Thomas Becket's bones was made by one of Thomas Derby's successors, William Thomas, who was clerk of the Privy Council from 1550.[8] Thomas, a mentor of the young Edward VI, was in or near Bologna in 1547 when news of the death of Henry VIII reached Italy. In the course of a heated discussion with some Italian gentlemen about the late king, Thomas defended Henry's character and policies, and he later wrote a narrative (*Il Pellegrino Inglese*) based upon the discussion in which an imaginary English pilgrim talks to some Italians about the king's behaviour in 1538.[9] In one of the English translations of the narrative, the pilgrim is asked the question that often arose on the continent in the years following the destruction of Becket's shrine:

'The poore St Thomas of Canterburye, alas it sufficed hym [the king] not [only] to spoyle and devour the great ryches of his shryne, whos treasure amounted to so manye thousand crownes; but to be avenged on the dead corpse dyd he not cause his bones openly to be burned?'[10]

In reply, the pilgrim recites a long litany of the superstitious and deceitful things that had been perpetrated by the monks at Canterbury, including their sales pitch that the blood-coloured water from a spring which had been doctored with red ochre was the blood of the holy martyr. Having thus prepared his ground, the pilgrim continues:

'The kyng ... could no lesse do then [than] deface the shrine that was the Auther of so much ydolatry. Whether the doing thereof hath bene the undoing of the canonised saint or not, I cannot tell. Butt this is true, that the bones are spred amongst the bones of so many dead men, that without some greate Miracle they wyll not be founde agayne.'

Many commentators have found this extract from *Il Pellegrino Inglese* to be an important, though not decisive, witness for the survival and burial of St Thomas's relics. Arthur Mason was among those impressed by it. 'It may be doubted', he wrote in 1920, 'whether William Thomas had a first-hand and independent knowledge of the facts, but he had been trained in the traditions of Cromwell and was steeped in the official atmosphere of Henry's reign; and his virtual denial of the burning of the bones has more than ordinary significance'.[11] But if the bones really were buried, as probably happened also to those of St Cuthbert at Durham (Chapter Eight) and St Swithun at Winchester (Chapter Nine), is there anything to suggest where that might have been? The answer returns us to the 20th century and to the abiding interest of deans and chapters of Canterbury Cathedral in the fate of St Thomas's relics.

---

1 D. Erasmus, *Pilgrimages to St Mary of Walsingham and St Thomas of Canterbury*, trans. J.G. Nichols, Westminster, 1849, pp. 44–60.

2 J. Gairdner (ed), *Letters and Papers, Foreign and Domestic, on the Reign of Henry VIII*, London, 1893, XIV, part 1, 402. The extracts quoted here are from the Privy Council's original document and are reproduced in H.S. Milman, 'The Vanished Memorials of St Thomas of Canterbury', *Archaeologia*, 1892, 53, part 1, p. 222.

3 A.D.K. Hawkyard, 'Thomas Derby', in S.T. Bindoff (ed.), *The History of Parliament: The House of Commons 1509–1558*, London, 1982.

4 C.F. Routledge, 'The Bones of Archbishop Becket', *Archaeologia Cantiana*, 1895, XXI, p. 79.

5 A.J. Mason, *What Became of the Bones of St Thomas?*, Cambridge, 1920 p. 159.

6 Milman, *op cit*, p. 219.

7 J. Crook, *St Swithun: Patron Saint of Winchester Cathedral*, Winchester, 2010, p. 21.

8 D.L. Thomas, 'William Thomas', in *Dictionary of National Biography 1885–1900*, vol. 56.

9 For a brief history of William Thomas's narrative in its different translations see C. Shrank, *Writing the Nation in Reformation England, 1530–1580*, Oxford, 2004, pp. 108–109.

10 This version of the text is the one in the Cotton collection in the British Library. It is reproduced in Mason, *op cit*, p. 162.

11 Mason, *op cit*, pp. 162–163.

CHAPTER 11

THE WITNESS OF THE CANTERBURY CHAPTER: THE WESTERN CRYPT

The records of the two 16th-century clerks of the Privy Council, Thomas Derby and William Thomas, are important for their clear assertions that the relics of St Thomas Becket survived the destruction of his shrine in 1538 and were buried; but they are less than helpful in indicating where that might have been (Chapter Ten). Derby wrote that the bones were 'buried in a noble towre', Thomas that they were 'spred amongst the bones of so many dead men, that without some greate Miracle they wyll not be founde agayne.' Speculation about the possible resting place of Becket's bones on the basis of these two reports would be futile. They are far too vague to have any value. The same cannot be said, however, of the actions of the Canterbury Cathedral authorities in the 1940s, 1950s and 1960s whose continuing fascination with the relics of St Thomas took them to two very specific locations in the crypt. The first, which has already appeared in the story (Chapter Six), was the northern transept of the western crypt which houses the apsidal chapels of St Mary Magdalene and St Nicholas.

The dean and chapter's interest in the western crypt as the possible resting place of Becket's bones originated in the early 1940s when, according to a story that came into the public domain in the late 1990s, the southern-most of the two ledger slabs in the chapels of St Mary Magdalene and St Nicholas in the northern transept was lifted. The pitted and broken slab, which is now in two parts joined by a modern concrete infill, looks to have been disturbed in the not-too-distant past. Three sides of it are sealed with a modern sealant, suggesting that its northern edge was used as a fulcrum to lift it like the hinged lid of a long box. It may have been in the course of this manoeuvre that the slab was damaged and had to be in-filled when it was laid back.

Stories about the lifting of this slab in the 1940s had been circulating in Canterbury for many years, but they did not come into the public domain (and therefore could not be quoted) until 1997 when *The Sunday Times* reported an interview it had conducted with Mr Cecil Humphery-Smith, a noted local expert on heraldry and genealogy whose association with Canterbury Cathedral went back to the Second World War.[1] The godson of the Venerable Julian Bickersteth, archdeacon of Maidstone from 1942, Humphery-Smith recalled in the interview how, as a young boy, his godfather had told him of being present when the slab was raised in about 1943 and objects were seen that persuaded him (Bickersteth) that he was looking at the remains of St Thomas Becket. Among the objects (according to Humphery-Smith's recollection of what his godfather had told him) were the bones of a very tall man, the fragments of an episcopal robe, and Becket's seal ring.

It is of no great consequence whether or not the dean and chapter were persuaded by Archdeacon Bickersteth's claims (though Bickersteth had had a distinguished career before coming to Canterbury and the dean at the time, Hewlett Johnson, held him in high regard).[2] The important fact is that, for whatever reason, the chapter believed from the mid-1940s

ABOVE: Chapel of St Nicholas in the western crypt of Canterbury Cathedral showing the broken ledger slab.

onwards that the relics of Thomas Becket were lying beneath this slab in the chapels of St Mary Magdalene and St Nicholas. So confident were they in their belief that they were prepared publicly to back it with hard cash. The process began in the autumn of 1946 when the chapter consulted Mr G.B. Beadle of Faith Craft-Works Ltd about the possibility of 'marking the burial place of St Thomas' with some coloured posts and cords.[3] Beadle submitted a design for the chapter's approval in October 1946,[4] but it was not accepted and the involvement of Faith Craft-Works in the project came to an abrupt halt. The chapter's belief in the authenticity of the grave lived on, however, and the project resurfaced eighteen months later in May 1948 when negotiations began with Messrs Seely and Paget for an altogether more opulent memorial (Chapter Six).

The timing of the chapter's approach to Seely and Paget was wholly extraordinary, confirming that this was rather more than the vanity project of a Trollopian archdeacon. Canterbury, like so many other towns and cities that had been devastated by German bombing in the war, was struggling to get back onto its feet as it faced the daunting task of restoring its shattered streets and buildings. The cathedral itself had largely been spared, but there was still much to be done with the very limited amount of money that was available. Superficial damage to the stonework

ABOVE: Canterbury and the cathedral in the aftermath of German air raids, 1942.

needed repairing; the medieval glass that had been removed in 1938 for safekeeping had to be reinstalled; the earthworks that had been built up in the quire and crypt required clearing; and many buildings in the precincts had to be renovated or rebuilt. The total cost was estimated to be £400,000 – the equivalent of about fourteen million pounds today. For the dean and chapter to think of spending their scarce resources at such a critical time on an expensive and controversial memorial to mark the final resting place of Becket's bones was almost unbelievable; but that is exactly what they did. They must have been very sure indeed that the bones were there.

The course of the negotiations with Seely and Paget following the initial contact in May 1948 is well documented (Chapter Six). In June of that year the architects were commissioned to prepare a design for the memorial,[5] and a letter to the dean and chapter in August spoke of their progress in creating a structure 'to protect the believed resting place of Becket's bones'. In October 1948 the watercolour sketch of the design for the northern transept was submitted to the chapter for its consideration.[6] So far so good; but then, with the project in the *western* crypt apparently progressing well, the dean and chapter suddenly decided in February 1949 to reopen the 1888 grave in the *eastern* crypt and ask Professor Cave to see if the bones that it contained might be those of St Thomas. Why? How can such a dramatic change of focus be explained?

The minutes of the chapter meeting at which the decision was taken to reopen the 1888 grave point to the likely answer. According to the Chapter Acts, it came after a letter had been read out from Mr Alfred Emden, the principal of St Edmund Hall at Oxford University and a distinguished historian.[7] Emden was a former colleague and long-standing friend of Canon John Shirley, the headmaster of the King's School and a member of the chapter. It was probably to Shirley that Emden had written the letter, and it was Shirley who was later asked by the chapter to consult Professor Cave about the reopening of the 1888 grave and the identification of the bones.

ABOVE: Mr Alfred Emden.

The letter from Alfred Emden has disappeared, but it is not too difficult to imagine what it might have said that persuaded the chapter, now in advanced talks with Seely and Paget about the memorial in the northern transept of the *western* crypt, to switch their attention to the 1888 grave in the *eastern* crypt. Emden must have known what the chapter was planning to do, and as an historian with an interest in Canterbury he must also have been well aware of the conclusion that Canon Arthur Mason had reached almost thirty years earlier about the authenticity of the 1888 bones. An obvious question must surely have formed in his mind: was it *really* wise for the Canterbury chapter to press ahead with their plans for the western crypt when the true relics of Becket might be lying in another grave only a short distant away? Would it not be prudent for the chapter to assure itself that an embarrassing and costly error was not about to be made? Emden may even have advised the chapter to commission a re-examination of the 1888 bones, for that is precisely what the chapter did.

There is no clearly documented evidence of the exact moment when the contract with Seely and Paget was terminated, but it must have been in the period between the reopening of the 1888 grave in July 1949 and the receipt of Professor Cave's report two years later. It is certainly the case that all connections with the company had ceased by the time the bones were reinterred in June 1951. The reasons for the chapter's dwindling enthusiasm for the memorial (having already invested a not inconsiderable amount of time and money in the project) are unclear. Canon Shirley's article in *The Times* in August 1951 sent a strong signal that the cathedral authorities were no longer as fascinated as they had been by the prospect of finding the relics.[8] Events had moved on, and there were other pressing matters to attend to. Moreover, the post-war membership of the Canterbury chapter was beginning to change, and the new canons coming in had not lived through the disorienting days of the early 1940s when things may have been done that would have looked very different through fresh post-war eyes. Yet this was not quite the end of the cathedral clergy's engagement with the chapels of St Mary Magdalene and St Nicholas, for while the chapter collectively may have lost interest in them, two of its members who had been most closely identified with the project – Canon John Shirley and Archdeacon Julian Bickersteth – had not.

The documented facts reveal a telling sequence of events. In May 1951 the dean and chapter received the report from Professor Cave showing conclusively that the bones he examined were not those of Becket (Chapter Seven). In the following month the chapter recorded its final minute on the matter.[9] At the *very next* meeting of the chapter in July 1951, John Shirley raised the question of replacing the altars in the chapels of St Mary Magdalene and St Nicholas.[10] For the next seven years, from the summer of 1951 onwards, work proceeded on the refurbishment

ABOVE: Chapels of St Mary Magdalene and St Nicholas in the western crypt of Canterbury Cathedral showing the broken ledger slab in the left foreground.

of the two chapels, and the Chapter Acts record the progress that was made. Part of the cost was borne personally by John Shirley and Julian Bickersteth. Shirley donated the altar in St Mary Magdalene together with the altar crucifix and a red sanctuary lamp (the liturgical colour of martyrdom). Bickersteth and his brothers furnished the adjacent chapel of St Nicholas and donated the altar in thanksgiving for their parents' long association with Canterbury. When Canon Shirley died in July 1967 his ashes were interred in St Mary Magdalene. A plaque marks the spot.

Was it merely a coincidental desire to enhance the fabric of the northern transept that led these two prominent members of the post-war chapter to turn their personal attention back to the two chapels in the immediate aftermath of Professor Cave's report? Or was Cave's verdict on the 1888 bones the key that opened the way for them to act upon what Bickersteth, at least, seems to have believed all along – that the chapels were intimately connected with Becket and that one of the graves was harbouring his bones? A former resident of the cathedral precincts who knew both Shirley and Bickersteth well has testified in personal correspondence with the author that the two men had paid for much of the refurbishment of the chapels *'out of veneration to the saint'* (original emphasis). These words must be treated with caution, for the writer is now dead and, since he never placed his testimony in the public domain, he cannot be named; but his long association with Shirley and Bickersteth clearly led him to believe that this was their true motivation.

Of course, the deep and sincere holding of a belief does not make it correct. Canon Shirley and Archdeacon Bickersteth may genuinely have believed the relics of Becket to be in the northern transept of the western crypt and yet may genuinely have been wrong. There is no decisive evidence one way or the other. Yet the fact that these two members of the chapter began a generous and on-going interest in that part of the crypt in the immediate aftermath of the Cave report suggests that they probably did believe that something was there.

Where does all of this leave the chapels of St Mary Magdalene and St Nicholas as a possible site for the location of St Thomas's bones? The related strands of evidence are suggestive but they have never been properly tested. There is Archdeacon Bickersteth's account, given to his godson Cecil Humphery-Smith and made public in 1997, of the lifting of the pitted and fractured slab in about 1943; there is the dean and chapter's astonishing pursuit of an elaborate and expensive memorial in the late 1940s to 'protect the believed resting place of Becket's bones'; and there is the unattributable testimony of a former colleague of Shirley and Bickersteth that, in personally funding much of the refurbishment of the chapels of St Mary Magdalene and St Nicholas in the 1950s, they were honouring what they believed to be the saint's final resting place.

None of this is conclusive, but it would be wrong to dismiss it merely as the flights of fancy of one or two imaginative members of the cathedral community who might have had an overly romantic view of things. After all, those who were present at the reopening of the 1888 grave in the eastern crypt in July 1949 *must* have known why they were there. They must, in other words, have been well aware of the chapter's plans for the memorial in the western crypt and of the importance of checking that a ghastly mistake was not about to be made there. They would surely have known that this was the real reason why Professor Cave and Dr Trevor had been asked to investigate whether the 1888 bones could be those of St Thomas.

Importantly, these witnesses to the reopening of the 1888 grave were by no means a small group of conspirators in league with the chapter, for as well as Cave and Trevor (who had presumably been chosen precisely for their academic objectivity) they included the cathedral agent, Mr Reginald Tophill; the cathedral architect, Mr Harold Anderson; and the cathedral librarian, Dr William Urry. Would any of these men, especially William Urry whose meticulous scholarship and knowledge of local history was legendary, have been there if they had really thought the project in the western crypt was fundamentally misguided? Would they not have communicated their reservations to the chapter long before any money was shelled out on architects' or consultants' fees?

In the end, of course, the dean and chapter more or less got the answer they wanted: although the 1888 bones could not be dated with any accuracy, Professor Cave was able to produce a multitude of other evidence to show that they could not possibly have been those of the saint. The way was now clear for the chapter to press confidently ahead with the project in the western crypt; but that didn't happen. Instead, Canon Shirley wrote his largely negative article in *The Times*; the chapter terminated the contract with Seely and Paget; the public forgot about the bones in the eastern crypt; John Shirley and Julian Bickersteth went ahead with their refurbishment of the chapels of St Mary Magdalene and St Nicholas in the western crypt; and Alexander Cave lived just long enough to ensure that his report did not disappear down the tubes of history.

Yet this is still not the end of the twisted tale, for in 1966 the grave in the eastern crypt was entered yet again. This time, though, it was done differently.

---

[1] C. Morgan and A. Alderson, 'Becket's bones kept secretly at Canterbury for 460 years', *The Sunday Times*, 22 June 1997, p. 3.

[2] J.R. Butler, *The Red Dean of Canterbury: The Public and Private Faces of Hewlett Johnson*, London, 2011, p. 104.

[3] Canterbury Cathedral Chapter Acts, 12 October 1946.

[4] Canterbury Cathedral Chapter Acts, 2 November 1946.

[5] Canterbury Cathedral Chapter Acts, 4 June 1948.

[6] Messrs Seely and Paget Architects, *A suggested treatment for the tomb of St Thomas of Canterbury: A proposal within the crypt of Canterbury Cathedral*, London, 1948. The receipt of the sketch is recorded in Canterbury Cathedral Chapter Acts, 2 October 1948.

[7] Canterbury Cathedral Chapter Acts, 5 February 1949.

[8] F.J. Shirley, 'Scientists' Examination of Canterbury Bones', *The Times*, 4 August 1951.

[9] Canterbury Cathedral Chapter Acts, 23 June 1951.

[10] Canterbury Cathedral Chapter Acts, 14 July 1951.

CHAPTER 12

THE WITNESS OF THE CANTERBURY CHAPTER: THE EASTERN CRYPT

ABOVE: Dr William Urry, who was present when the '1888 grave' was entered in both 1949 and 1966.

Officially, the re-entry into the 1888 grave in the eastern crypt in 1966 never took place. There is no mention of it in the Chapter Acts and cathedral officials have never commented publicly on it; but it did happen, as one of those who was present at the time, Mr Bill Urry, publicly attested thirty years later.[1] Mr Urry revealed that his father, Dr William Urry, who at that time was the cathedral archivist, had obtained the agreement of the dean and chapter to 'the excavation of an area of the eastern crypt ... in a quest to find [Becket's] bones'; and his son accompanied him on the dig. The initiative was seemingly William Urry's own and, according to his son, 'his infectious enthusiasm fired even the initially surly workman assigned to the task'. William Urry's continuing interest in the grave as late as the mid-1960s is puzzling, for he would obviously have known that the bones were not those of Becket. He had, after all, taken a leading part in the opening of the grave in July 1949 and he must have been involved in all the subsequent dealings with Professor Cave. Why might he have wanted to enter the grave yet again?

On this occasion the grave was entered in an unusual way, as a casual glance at it reveals. Unlike in 1888 and 1949 when the slab above the grave was removed and the coffin exposed, the operation in 1966 took an entirely different form. A six-foot pit was dug at the south-eastern corner, just large enough to accommodate a right-handed man with a spade, and the grave was then entered laterally *underneath* the stone coffin. The coffin itself, which had not been raised in either 1888 or 1949, was untouched and the covering slab remained in place, with most of the sealant around it visibly undisturbed from its closure in 1951 apart from a small section adjacent to the pit. When the pit was filled in at the end of the 1966 dig, the cement was of a different colour and texture to the surrounding floor of the crypt. So too was the small length of sealant. The differences are immediately and obviously apparent.

What might have been the purpose of this singular manoeuvre? There are two possible answers, both of which had been discussed on several occasions following the discovery of the grave in 1888. The first is that, if the coffin had indeed been set up as a decoy (Chapter Nine), then the true relics of St Thomas Becket might have been buried beneath it. If, in other words, the monks had succeeded in protecting their precious treasure and needed rapidly to find a place for its concealment where the king's commissioners would be unlikely to look, the space beneath a decoy coffin might be an audacious – if risky – hideaway. The monks might have reasoned that if the decoy coffin did its job and its contents were destroyed by the commissioners in the false belief that they were the true relics, then there would have been no incentive for them to look any further. If, on the other hand, the decoy failed to convince, then it might not have occurred to the commissioners to continue looking in the same place.

If this was the thinking behind the 1966 dig it was not an entirely fanciful idea. There is evidence that the same thing happened in other places, most strikingly in Durham Cathedral where the relics of St Cuthbert were removed from his shrine on the orders of Henry VIII in 1539. The relics may – or may not – have been exchanged for decoy bones during the two years they were kept in a revestry in the cathedral, but whether they were the genuine articles or not, the bones were buried in a new grave dug beneath the erstwhile site of Cuthbert's shrine (Chapter Eight). When this grave was opened in May 1827, the skeleton that was generally assumed to be that of St Cuthbert was found in the *bottom* of three coffins stacked one upon another. The other two coffins contained an assortment of bones, some of which could have come from important personages.[2]

Whether or not the stacking had been done in a deliberate attempt to conceal St Cuthbert's remains is a secondary consideration. The important conclusion to be drawn from the events at Durham is that sacred relics (or what were believed to be sacred relics) were interred at the bottom of a grave containing multiple coffins. A similar thing happened at Oxford Cathedral where the relics of St Frideswide were buried with the remains of Catherine Martyr, the wife of one of the cathedral canons.[3] There is no reason to suppose that the monks of Canterbury could not have carried out a similar deception. A multi-layered burial of the kind that was used at Durham might also explain the very shallow depth of the top coffin in the 1888 grave – only three inches beneath the level of the crypt floor, according to the original report. There may simply not have been enough room to go any deeper.

Is this what William Urry was looking for in 1966? If so, he must have thought there was a possibility that the relics of St Thomas had survived the destruction of the shrine in 1538, for otherwise he would not have sought the consent of the dean and chapter to look for them. Indeed, being familiar with Professor Cave's account of the strange history of the bones discovered in 1888, Urry may even have considered the possibility that the coffin had been set up as a decoy. There may, however, be an entirely different reason for the curious nature of the dig in 1966 that has nothing whatsoever to do with Becket or his relics. The clue is found in a letter that Canon John Shirley wrote to William Urry in January 1952, six months after the 1888 bones had returned from Professor Cave's laboratory in London and been reburied in the eastern crypt. In the letter, Shirley asked Urry whether anything was known about the age at death of William de Audeville, the 12th-century abbot of the great Benedictine monastery of Evesham in Worcestershire.[4] What was this all about?

Abbot de Audeville was a former monk of Canterbury Cathedral who died in the city in January 1159 while on a visit to the archbishop, Theobald. The circumstances of his burial in the crypt of the cathedral were recorded in the *Chronicles of the Abbots of Evesham*, published in the Rolls Series.

> 'He [de Audeville] lies buried at the head of the blessed Thomas the Martyr, who before he went there by reason of a visitation, when he was visited there by the Lord [that is, he died] saw in dreams, as he reported

ABOVE: The '1888 grave' in the eastern crypt showing the pit that was dug in the course of the 1966 excavation.

to the brethren, that the sun had been buried at his feet. Which vision received its interpretation in process of time, after the blessed Thomas was buried at his feet.'[5]

De Audeville's death in Canterbury in 1159 took place almost twelve years before Becket's when the eastern crypt would have had no special significance; but following Becket's burial there in December 1170 the abbot's body was now (according to the *Chronicles*) 'buried at the head of the blessed Thomas the Martyr'. Becket's tomb was located a few feet to the east of the 1888 grave, which would mean that de Audeville's coffin was now lying 'at his [Becket's] head' – that is, in the 1888 grave. Knowing this, as he surely did, William Urry may have been intrigued by the idea that the coffer discovered in 1888 had been inserted into the grave *above* that of de Audeville. This would certainly account for Urry's interest in seeing whether there was a second coffin beneath it, but it would not have shed any further light onto his 'quest to find Becket's bones' (as his son put it in his letter to the *Kentish Gazette* in 1995).

In fact, John Shirley's question to William Urry in January 1952 did not require the 1888 grave to be re-entered at all: he had merely asked whether anything was known about de Audeville's age at the time of his death. Coming so soon after Professor Cave's report in 1951, Shirley may have been wondering whether the 1888 bones were actually those of the abbot. Whatever

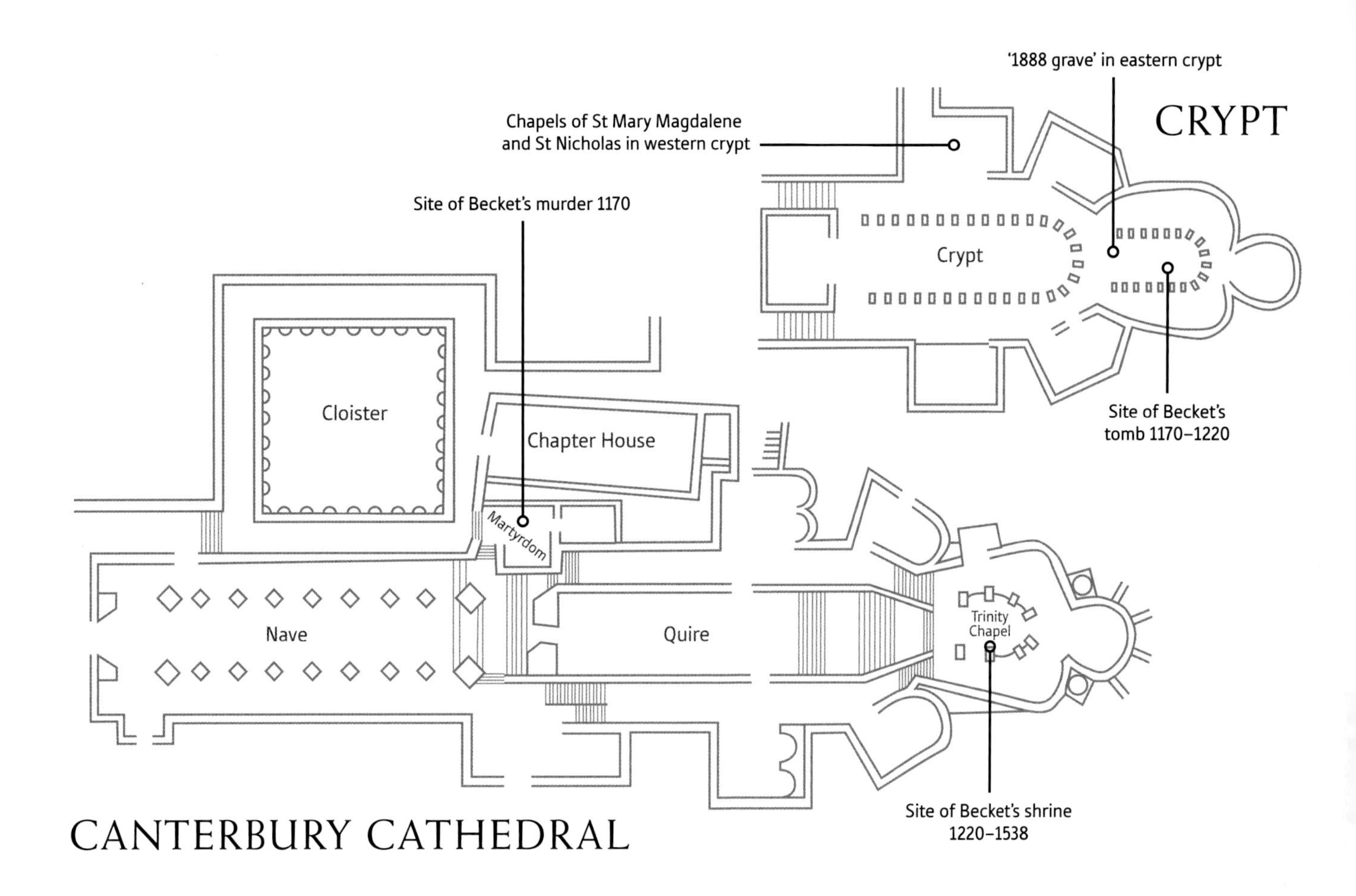

ABOVE: **Plan of Canterbury Cathedral showing the sites associated with Becket.**

William Urry's reply (which is unknown), it is highly unlikely that the bones could be those of de Audeville, for Cave had demonstrated very clearly in his report that the cadaver had originally been buried in bare earth and later dug up with great haste and carelessness. Such a double indignity would surely not have been inflicted on a visiting abbot from one of the great Benedictine monasteries of the day.

The obvious question arising from the 1966 incursion into the grave in the eastern crypt is whether anything was found? The public has never been told, for it was not an official operation and, apart from the fact that it actually took place, nothing has leaked out about it. The silence could be consistent with two entirely opposite outcomes: either nothing was found, in which case there was nothing to leak, or something suggestive of the relics was found, in which case the cathedral authorities may by this time have had good reason for keeping it quiet. It would be a welcome contribution to the 800th anniversary of the translation of St Thomas's relics if the cathedral authorities were to reveal to the public why the dig was authorised in 1966 and what, if anything, was found.

---

1 W.R. Urry, letter in the *Kentish Gazette*, 9 February 1995. Mr Urry expanded briefly on some factual points about the excavation in a letter to the author dated 16 February 1995.

2 D. Willem, *St Cuthbert's Corpse: A Life After Death*, Durham, 2013, pp. 63–66.

3 J. Blair, *St Frideswide: Patron of Oxford*, London, 2004.

4 Canterbury Cathedral Archives, Add. MS 313.

5 Quoted in M. Beazeley, *The Canterbury Bones*, London, 1913, p. 23.

CHAPTER 13

WHERE IS THOMAS BECKET BURIED?

Among the questions most frequently asked by visitors to Canterbury Cathedral is the place of Thomas Becket's burial. Judgements have to be made by guides and assistants about the most appropriate way of answering it. For some visitors it is sufficient to explain that there are no authentic records of the destruction of Becket's shrine in September 1538 and that consequently the fate of his relics is unknown. Others, however, are more persistent: surely *something* must be known? The problem then is to judge how much of this intriguing tale to tell. Commonly, visitors are eager to hear too much rather than too little.

This book has tried to narrate the story to the extent that it is currently known. All the important facts are fully referenced, allowing others to check the credibility of the sources and the way the evidence has been used to fashion the story. There are, of course, many missing pieces in the puzzle and a certain amount of theorising has had to be done to cover the gaps. Nevertheless, the book has been at pains to explore both sides of the various questions that have arisen. The evidence has been allowed to speak for itself, and the evidence is conflicting. Did Becket's relics survive the despoliation of his shrine in 1538? Were his bones burnt or were they somehow kept safe? Was the 1888 grave in the eastern crypt deliberately constructed as a decoy to mislead King Henry's commissioners? Do the true relics lie near the chapels of St Mary Magdalene and St Nicholas in the western crypt? There are no straightforward answers.

The fact that the evidence is inconclusive is important, for it means that nobody in the debates since 1888 can rightly lay claim to know the truth. This has not, of course, prevented them from doing so: the 'believers' and the 'sceptics' from the original 19th-century controversies still have their modern counterparts, accepting only the evidence that fits their own particular agendas and dismissing anything that contradicts them. Those who have examined the evidence and are undecided in which direction it should take them are relatively sparse on the ground.

The modern telling of the story of the relics of Thomas Becket begins with the grave that was accidentally discovered in the eastern crypt in January 1888. From what is now known about it, it can reasonably be explained as a decoy grave constructed by the monks in 1538 to deflect the attention of the king's commissioners away from the true location of the relics. This may not be the correct explanation, but no better alternative has yet emerged that takes account of *all* the known facts. The grave is there in Canterbury Cathedral and it cannot simply be wished away. It must have got there through a particular set of actions at a particular point in time, and it is entirely proper to wonder what those actions might have been.

It follows from the decoy theory that the monks must at least have *tried* to deceive the king's commissioners when they arrived in Canterbury in September 1538. Whether they succeeded is an entirely separate matter, but try they seemingly did – as also did their Benedictine counterparts in other monastic cathedrals in England. Such actions are hardly surprising: it is

ABOVE: A Tudor blacksmith at work.

far more credible to imagine communities of monks preparing to guard their sacred treasures, if necessary to the point of death, than it is to picture them standing idly by, waiting for the king's men to come and carry out their sacrilegious purposes. They would, moreover, have had little reason to suppose that the royal hostility towards them would be anything other than temporary. From their perspective, the king might soon be dead, and his Catholic daughter Mary (who could very well succeed him) would be far more sympathetic towards the veneration of the saints. All that was necessary was for the relics to be kept safe until that happened.

The question of whether or not Becket's bones were burnt is obviously crucial to any consideration of their possible survival: if they were destroyed in this way, as many believe, then that is the end of the matter. Rumours to that effect were undoubtedly circulating in the aftermath of the shrine's destruction in 1538, and in time the rumours came to be accepted as fact: Becket's bones *were* burnt, probably inside the cathedral, and the ashes *were* disposed of, albeit in different ways. Such stories, however, are difficult to reconcile with physical realities. Bones do not burn easily and they do not burn completely to ash. A human skeleton would need to be exposed to a fire of between 1,000 and 1,500 degrees centigrade for about ninety minutes before it is fully degraded into bony fragments. Temperatures in this range and for this duration could certainly have been achieved in a Tudor blacksmith's forge, but they are rather less likely to have been attained in a hastily prepared bonfire inside the cathedral using whatever fuel was conveniently to hand. Even if it could have been done, a fire of such intensity and duration would have left significant burn marks on the fabric of the cathedral; yet there are no signs of any such damage at the site of Becket's shrine where (according to one account) the burning had taken place.

Because of these physical realities, the stories of the burning of Becket's bones must be treated with caution; and there are other reasons too for holding reservations about them. No eye-witness accounts have surfaced of any bonfire of bones in Canterbury. It is true that in both October and December 1538 Pope Paul III accused King Henry of *ordering* the burning of the bones, and the accusations appear to have been circulated widely on the continent; but there is no public record of any papal claim that they had *actually* been burnt. Yet once Pope Paul had launched the charge against Henry, few people in Europe would have been inclined to draw a distinction between the command and the deed.

Even if all these difficulties are set aside and it is accepted that a bonfire of the necessary intensity *did* take place inside the cathedral, there can be no certainty that the bones of St Thomas Becket were thrown onto it. There were dozens – perhaps scores – of assorted relics in the cathedral that had been shown to generations of pilgrims, and burning them would have been an obvious and convenient way of disposing of them. There is also the possibility, hinted at in Thomas Derby's entry in the Privy Council record in 1539, that it was the counterfeit skull of Becket that had been burnt, not the one removed from the shrine. Such a conflagration of bogus relics would have been wholly to the liking of the king.

As the stories of burning developed and spread, imaginative splashes of detail were woven into them. The stories circulating on the continent all stressed that after the bones had been burnt, the ashes were scattered to the winds; but no such vivid detail appears in the English chronicles. Instead, they dwell upon the finding of the skull in the shrine and the consequent exposure of the fraud that had been perpetrated on generations of pilgrims. When the Greek traveller Nicander Nucius arrived in Canterbury in 1545 he picked up a story that the ashes from the burning had been fired through the barrel of a cannon. Others claimed they had been dumped in the nearby River Stour. Not only do these stories conflict with each other, they falter in the light of the fact that human bones can only be turned into ash by pulverising the bony fragments that would remain from a fire; yet there is no mention in the records of any such grinding taking place.

Against the stories of the burning of Becket's bones must be set other contemporary voices that hint at something different. Thomas Derby, the clerk of the Privy Council at the time who was well placed to know what had happened, asserted that the bones had been 'taken away and bestowed in suche place as the same shuld cause no superstition afterwards'; and William Thomas, a slightly later clerk of the Privy Council, wrote that they had been 'spred amongst the bones of so many dead men, that without some greate Miracle they wyll not be founde

ABOVE: Burning of John Wycliffe's exhumed bones at Lutterworth, 1428.

agayne'. The clearest signal that nothing destructive was done to St Thomas's relics came from the traditionalist Bishop of Winchester, Stephen Gardiner, who passed through Canterbury in the immediate aftermath of the destruction of the shrine in September 1538 and was reported as saying that he did not dislike what had been done there. Indeed, he went so far as to hope that the relics of St Swithun in Winchester Cathedral had been accorded the same treatment. It seems all but inconceivable that Bishop Gardiner would have expressed such a view if he had known that Becket's bones had been burnt or otherwise destroyed.

Taking all of the evidence into account, and allowing for its errors and omissions, two statements can be made that are consistent with the facts that are currently available. First, it is more likely than not that the monks of Canterbury Cathedral took steps to prevent the desecration of the relics of St Thomas, and second, it is more likely than not that the relics themselves survived the destruction of his shrine. Whether there is a causal connection between these two conclusions is entirely unknown: the survival of the relics could have resulted from events *other than* any action that may have been taken by the monks. The fact that the decoy grave was seemingly not required to do what it was set up to do could be explained by the fact that the king's commissioners were under instructions to bury the relics in a quiet place where they would no longer be a focus of Catholic piety. Such was the documented fate of saintly relics in other cathedrals in England, and the same could have happened at Canterbury. If so, then any preparations that the monks may have made to deceive the commissioners would have been rendered redundant, and the commissioners would have had no reason to be scrabbling around in the crypt.

There is, however, an enormous gulf between accepting that the relics of St Thomas *could* have survived and imagining where they might now be lying. Here, the conclusions that can be drawn from the available evidence are flimsy. The observations of the two Privy Council clerks, Thomas Derby and William Thomas, are useless. Indeed, if William Thomas was correct in asserting that the bones of the saint were 'spred amongst the bones of so many dead men', that is the end of the matter. They will 'not be founde agayne'.

This apart, the only other clues are those that have been proposed by the cathedral authorities themselves. There is well documented evidence that in the late 1940s the dean and chapter strongly believed that Becket's bones were in one of the graves adjacent to the chapels of St Mary Magdalene and St Nicholas in the north transept of the western crypt; and when the chapter's belief in this began to falter in 1951 the baton of faith was taken up by two of its members who contributed personally to the cost of refurbishing the chapels, probably as an act of piety towards St Thomas. Their convictions may or may not have been well founded: they have never been tested. The only other clue to the possible location of Becket's bones emerged in 1966 when the 1888 grave in the eastern crypt was entered yet again, this time in a very unusual way, in what was described as a quest to find the relics. On this occasion, however, the operation was unofficial and no information about it has come into the public domain.

And there, tantalisingly but inconclusively, the story almost comes to an end. But not quite, for if the story began with an elbow bone (Prologue) it is fitting that it should end with a tooth (Epilogue).

EPILOGUE: A TOOTH

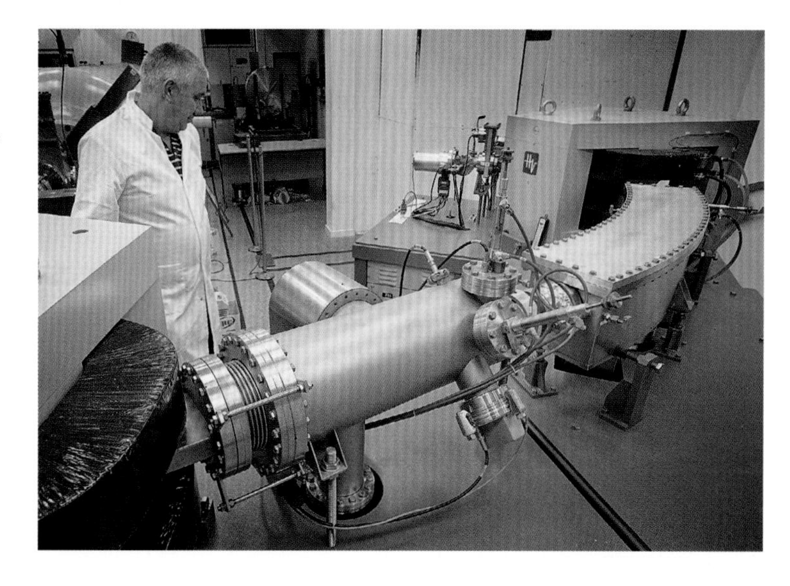

ABOVE: Oxford Radiocarbon Accelerator Unit.

Following Professor Alexander Cave's examination of the 1888 bones in his laboratory at St Bartholomew's Hospital Medical College between 1949 and 1951, they were returned to Canterbury and reburied at a little ceremony in the eastern crypt in June 1951. But not quite all of them were replaced in the coffin. One tooth (probably the right upper canine) remained on the surface, having been sent to Sweden in a registered envelope postmarked 'Cambridge, 2 January 1951'. The sender was Dr Jack Trevor, the Cambridge archaeologist who had been present when the 1888 grave was re-opened in July 1949 but whose name does not appear on any of the subsequent documentation apart from the envelope containing the tooth. It is reasonable to assume that, while most of the job of examining the bones was done by Professor Cave and his team in London, Dr Trevor was tasked with contacting a forensic dentist to see if any further light could be shed on the tooth – and, by implication, on the skeleton itself.

The recipient of the envelope and its curious content was Dr Gösta Gustafson of Malmö University, an acknowledged expert on dating the age of death from teeth.[1] No record exists of any report he may have submitted to Dr Trevor, and his work was not mentioned at all in Professor Cave's report. Dr Gustafson must have failed to return the tooth in time for its reburial with the rest of the bones in June 1951. When it did eventually come back to Cambridge, Dr Trevor forwarded it to Canon John Shirley in Canterbury, and he in turn passed it to the cathedral archivist, Dr William Urry.[2] With it came a handwritten note of explanation from Shirley. It is undated but could have been as late as the mid-1960s, shortly before his death.

> 'This is one of the four [sic] teeth which the skeleton in the East Crypt was found to have on the occasion of our opening the tomb. You might like it in the relics and treasures of the Library. I have guarded it all the time – and after all, it might be a Saint's tooth.'

S: DAVID
CAERLEON:

If the tooth has any current utility, it lies in the fact that the 1888 bones may be capable of being dated, using carbon-dating techniques, without resort to any further opening of the grave. There are precedents. In 1998 small samples of six bones that were believed to be those of St Chad at Birmingham were carbon-dated at the Oxford Radiocarbon Accelerator Unit.[3] The results showed that three of the six bones went back to the 7th century (St Chad died in 672) and probably came from the same individual. The others were also dated to the 7th century but seemed to have come from different individuals and could have been mixed up with those of the saint at any of a number of stages in the history of the relics. There was nothing in the report of the analysis to refute the hypothesis that the three associated bones were those of St Chad, and the author concluded that the rigorous scientific investigation of reputed relics was a 'worthy scholarly undertaking'.

A closer parallel to the Canterbury tooth would be the carbon-dating that was carried out in 1997, also at Oxford, on the supposed relics of St David, the patron saint of Wales.[4] The relics had been discovered a hundred years earlier in the walls of St David's Cathedral, since when they had been kept in a wooden casket in the cathedral with a note stating they were the bones of St David and St Justinian. The carbon-dating, however, showed them to be at least four hundred years later than the probable death of St David, falsifying the hypothesis about their authenticity. As at St David's, the carbon-dating of the 1888 tooth at Canterbury would contribute nothing to its positive identification, but it could cast doubt on the decoy theory if the tooth was found to be any later than, say, the last quarter of the 15th century (or whatever time is necessary for an earth burial to produce the grave-weathering that Professor Cave noted in his report in 1951). By extension, it would also cast doubt on the monks' hypothesised attempt to protect St Thomas's relics from the king's commissioners in 1538.

Since knowledge advances as much through falsification as through the more complex task of verification, the possibility that the carbon-dating of the tooth might falsify the decoy theory would be a very welcome contribution to the 800th anniversary of the translation of St Thomas Becket's relics. Questions would still remain, of course, but the answers would now have to be sought in different directions.

LEFT: **St David, by William Burges.**

---

1 G. Gustafson, 'Age of Determination of Teeth', *Journal of the American Dental Association*, 41, 1951.

2 The tooth and the envelope now reside in the Canterbury Cathedral Archives, Add. Ms 313.

3 A. Boyle, 'The Bones of the Anglo-Saxon Bishop and Saint, Chad: A Scientific Analysis', *Church Archaeology*, 1998, vol. 2, pp. 35–38.

4 R. Gledhill, 'Tests prove cathedral's bones are not St David', *The Times*, 1 March 1997, p. 15.

An imprint of Pavilion Books Company Limited.

Written by John Butler.
 Pictures reproduced with kind permission of Jim Styles: 2, 5, 31, 55, 58. Canterbury Cathedral Stained Glass Studios: 3, 4, 72. Shutterstock: 6. Esztergom Basilica: 7 left. Marie Lan-Nguyen: 7 right. Canterbury Cathedral Archives and Library: 8, 14 left, 63. Alamy: 9, 12, 13, 19, 33, 48, 49, 56, 65, 67, 69. British Library: 10, 16, 17, 21, 24, 39. Scala Archives: 11. Getty Images: 14 right, 20, 25 left. Courtesy of the author: 26, 29, 30, 62. The King's School Canterbury: 28. David Iliff: 52.

Designed by Lee-May Lim.
Cover photography by David Salmo.

ISBN: 978-1-84165-864-3 1/19

Printed in Turkey

Pitkin Publishing
Pavilion Books Company Limited
43 Great Ormond Street
London WC1N 3HZ

www.pavilionbooks.com